# XI JINPING'S ADAGES

---

## A GUIDE TO THE CHINESE LEADER'S CLASSICAL ALLUSIONS

*compiled by*

## PUBLICITY DEPARTMENT OF THE COMMUNIST PARTY OF CHINA

*in association with*

## CHINA MEDIA GROUP

ACA PUBLISHING LTD

Published by
ACA Publishing Ltd.
University House
11-13 Lower Grosvenor Place
London SW1W 0EX, UK
Tel: +44 (0)20 3289 3885
E-mail: info@alaincharlesasia.com
Web: www.alaincharlesasia.com

Beijing Office
Tel: +86 (0)10 8472 1250

Compiled by China Central Television
Translators: Hui Cooper and Dennis Cooper

Published by ACA Publishing Ltd in association with
People's Publishing House, Beijing, China

Paperback ISBN: 978-1-83890-000-7
eBook ISBN: 978-1-83890-001-4

A catalogue record for *Xi Jinping's Adages: A Guide to the Chinese Leader's Classical Allusions* is available from the National Bibliographic Service of the British Library.

# CONTENTS

PART XII

**WHEN THE GREAT WAY PREVAILS, ALL UNDER HEAVEN WILL BE ONE COMMUNITY**

# A NOTE FROM THE EDITOR

This book is based on a 2018 television special, broadcast on China Central Television to an audience of 441 million. Its title was 平语近人 (*Píng Yǔ Jìn Rén*), a clever play on words which roughly translates to *Xi Jinping's Language is Close to the People.*

The aim of the programme and its accompanying book was to shed light on the thoughts of the General Secretary as voiced in his key speeches, as well as to popularise the Chinese classics and emphasise the relevance of China's rich cultural heritage to the country's prospects as a modern nation.

*Xi Jinping's Adages*, our concise English edition of *Píng Yǔ Jìn Rén*, excerpts quotes from thirty-five of the speeches covered in the television special and pairs them with expert analysis transcribed from its screenplay. Reading this officially sanctioned analysis of the Chinese leader's classical allusions affords a unique and interesting perspective on the state of China today as the country reconciles itself with the cultural traditions, literary heritage and ancient philosophy it once rejected in the name of progress. This book shows how, in a way, things have come full circle. Education and tradition, once frowned upon by the CPC, are now held up as important prerequisites for the country's future development.

Beyond erudite explanation and analysis of classic aphorisms, this book teems with anecdotes about Xi Jinping's own life and how he has put the words of the sages into practice, be it as leader of the Party, figurehead of the nation or as a young man in the countryside undergoing education through labour.

So whether you're interested in China's culture and classics, its political and economic development, or the life and times of its paramount leader Xi Jinping, we believe this brief volume will satisfy your curiosity.

# A NOTE FROM THE CHINESE PUBLISHERS ON 'CULTURAL SELF-CONFIDENCE'

CULTURAL SELF-CONFIDENCE is a force that is more basic, goes deeper and lasts longer in the development of a country and a nation, and naturally the Chinese people's cultural self-confidence is closely linked to China's fine traditional culture. General Secretary Xi Jinping has emphasised previously that in the new era, the Chinese people need to promote Chinese culture and to realise its creative transformation and innovative development. In this respect, he himself has led by example. In a series of important speeches and articles that have left a deep impression on people, no matter whether talking about major issues of governing a country, or defining China's principles, viewpoints or positions on international occasions, or talking with cadres and the common people at grassroots level, he has frequently quoted pearls of wisdom from classical Chinese literature. Not only has he accurately interpreted the quintessential excellence of traditional Chinese culture, he has also added new connotations in keeping with the times, which shine with the ideological radiance of a new era. These quotations vividly blended with his plain language of the ordinary people, brings the characters in the classics back to life again.

**part one**

# Concern for Every Leaf on Every Branch

一枝一叶总关情

INTERPRETATION
IN PART I PROVIDED BY

-

**Professor Wang Liqun**
*Deputy Director of the Centre for the
System of Socialism with Chinese Characteristics Studies*

&

**Professor Guo Jianning**
*Deputy Director of the Research Centre for the Theoretical System
of Socialism with Chinese Characteristics, Peking University*

# ONE
## WHAT IS 'FOR THE PEOPLE'?

" Zheng Banqiao from the Qing dynasty was a well-known painter and a man of letters. He served for a long time as a magistrate in Fan county, Henan province and in Wei county, Shandong province. (As a magistrate), he attached importance to farming and sericulture and he aided the victims of natural disasters. In his office there was never any backlog of work on his desk, while at home none of his property was obtained by bribery. He was an incorruptible, upright and honest official, therefore he enjoyed public support. His poem *'In my magistrate's residence I lie listening to bamboo rustling, it sounds like the people moaning in distress. We may be modest as small county officials, but we are concerned for every leaf on every branch'* has become an eternal aspiration of loving the people."

— XI JINPING

THIS SPEECH WAS GIVEN by General Secretary Xi Jinping on 9 May 2014 when he participated in a meeting of the Party Standing Committee of Lankao county, Henan province, on the subject of democratic life, in which he alluded to a poem by Zheng Banqiao from the Qing dynasty. General Secretary Xi is particularly fond of this poem, so he has alluded to it on many occasions. Why does he attach such importance to this poem?

### According to **Professor Wang Liqun:**

This poem was written when Zheng Banqiao was the magistrate of Wei county in Shandong province. It has a rather long title - *Painting Bamboo for Governor Bao from the Magistrate's Residence in Wei County*. When it was composed, Wei county was experiencing a natural

3

disaster. What was Zheng Banqiao's solution for the problems related to the unfortunate victims' livelihood? He undertook a capital construction project and let the civilians engage in the building work. Anyone who took part in the construction work got paid and fed. This action solved the problem of victims starving due to the natural disaster, therefore the poem expressed Magistrate Zheng's deep feelings for the people.

TWO

# WHY 'FOR THE PEOPLE'?

*'Government thrives when it is exercised in accordance with the will of the people and declines when it goes against the will of the people.'* For a political party or a political power, its future and destiny ultimately depend on the will of the people."

— XI JINPING

ON 21 SEPTEMBER 2014, General Secretary Xi Jinping gave the above explanation at a meeting to celebrate the 65th anniversary of the establishment of the Chinese People's Political Consultative Conference (CPPCC).

### According to **Professor Wang Liqun:**

The two lines quoted here by General Secretary Xi are from the chapter on *Shepherding the People* (*Mumin*) of the *Guanzi*, which is a collection of related treatises and articles of Guan Zhong in the Spring and Autumn Period (770-476BC). The Four Acts of Submission to the Will of the People (*Sishun*) was a section of *Mumin* talking about how *"Political power thrives when it is exercised in accordance with the will of the people and declines when it goes against the will of the people."* The key point here is that popular support is the ultimate decisive factor for the rise and fall of state power.

Many ancient Chinese scholars understood this argument of Guan Zhong very well, particularly some of the grassroots-level officials. One official who was recorded in the *Biography of Tong Hui* in *The Book of the Later Han* illustrates this point. This official was called Tong Hui, who lived in the latter years of the East Han dynasty (25-220AD) and was appointed magistrate of Buqi county. The *Biography of Tong Hui* contains these words: "This area is peaceful and quiet, and the county prison has had no prisoners for many years running". This was a rarity! A county prison with no prisoners for many years meant that the county magistrate had done an excellent job in maintaining public order. Apart from public order, the citizens faced another problem, namely, tigers running rampant in the county. After Tong Hui took office, he found ways to drive the animals away into the mountains, so that the county was soon stabilised. Fan Ye, the compiler of *The History of the Later Han* wrote the following words in praise of Tong Hui: 'If those who are in power can understand and sympathise with the people, the sound of every family will be like happy music.' It means that when an official is loved by the common people, every family will be extremely happy. The rise and fall of a state lies in its support of the people, but whether a government receives public support or not depends on the conduct of its officials.

# THREE
## HOW TO CARE 'FOR THE PEOPLE'?

> 'Any policies that benefit the people, no matter how minor they seem, carry them all out; eradicate those, no matter how insignificant they are, that harm the people.' That is to say, no matter how trivial a policy is, as long as it benefits the common people, the government must implement it; but eliminate it if it harms the common people. History is written by the people, so we owe all our achievements to the people. So long as we are deeply rooted among the people and firmly rely on them, we will be able to obtain inexhaustible power and forge ahead courageously, come rain or shine."

— XI JINPING

### According to **Professor Wang Liqun:**

THESE TWO LINES quoted by General Secretary Xi are from the *Textual Study on the Rites of Zhou, (Zhou Guan Bian Fei)* written by the famous Qing economist Wan Sida (1633-1683). It says that any government policies that either benefit or harm the common people are important no matter how minor they are. Anything that benefits the people should be encouraged whereas anything that harms the people must be discarded.

There is a famous story to illustrate this viewpoint. Liu Chong was known in history as the 'One Coin Magistrate'. When he was an official, he loved his people very much. He attended to everything that would benefit the people but did all he could to eliminate anything that might harm them.

He did an excellent job in his post as the chief of Kuaiji prefecture, so he was promoted to the central government. On hearing that he was leaving, five or six old men went to see him off, each carrying a hundred coins.

When the old men saw Liu Chong, they told him that before he came to the county, the locals heard dogs barking at midnight or even the whole night. Why? Because those officials only waited until night fell when people were at home sleeping. They came to catch people and demand money, or to collect land taxes. In previous years, dogs barked every night. But since Liu Chong came to be the magistrate, no barking of dogs was heard at night, while the burden on the local farmers had eased tremendously. Now he was leaving, they could not keep him, so they brought the money to show their gratitude. Magistrate Liu was very touched by the old men's gesture. He said that if he refused to accept the money, he would be refusing a token of their respect but if he accepted it, it would be too much. Therefore, he suggested that he accept one coin from them. This one coin represented the devotion of his entire energy and thought to promoting the well-being of the common people, and his wholehearted efforts to stop evil officials from extorting people's wealth. This one coin made him as rich as Croesus and represented great wealth.

## According to **Professor Guo Jianning:**

History is a mirror that we must draw lessons from. We, the broad masses of the people, including young students, and particularly Party members and cadres, should study history and acquaint ourselves with China's several thousand years' history of civilisation, the history of our Party and the country, from which we draw wisdom and experience of governance so that we can make a greater contribution to society and the country.

But how to be for the people? It is to seek happiness for the people and do more good deeds for the public.

China's socialism with Chinese characteristics has entered a new era. The principal contradiction in our society has evolved into the contradiction between the increasing demand for a better life for the people, and unbalanced development and underdevelopment. So how do we adapt to this change? At present the most important task is to secure a decisive victory in building China into an all-round moderately prosperous society.

General Secretary Xi Jinping has talked a lot about this task, whether about "true poverty alleviation and to alleviate true poverty", or "targeted poverty alleviation and targeted liberation of people from poverty", or "not one less in the process of building an all-round moderately prosperous society and not a single soul should be left behind on the path to collective prosperity".

The concept of "targeted poverty alleviation" was first put forward by General Secretary Xi Jinping during his inspection tour of Shibadong village.

Whether China can become moderately prosperous, what really counts is the lives of the country's villagers. General Secretary Xi Jinping pointed out in one of his speeches that by 2020, under the present standard, we will realise the target of lifting China's poverty-stricken population out of poverty, and this is our solemn promise. After he had finished saying this, he emphasised that "he is true to his word". By 2020, tens of millions of poverty-stricken Chinese will be lifted out of poverty and impoverished counties will rid themselves of the label of being poor counties. So let us make joint efforts to accomplish this historical undertaking, an undertaking of great significance for the Chinese nation and the whole world.

The policy of targeted poverty alleviation and building an all-round moderately prosperous society embodies the concentrated purpose of our Party to serve the people wholeheartedly and General Secretary Xi Jinping's people-centred philosophy of development.

Making development people-centric is the important content and distinguishing feature of Xi Jinping Thought, which has substantial content and profound ideas, as well as many valuable sayings. For instance, "Rely on the people to create great historical achievements, and lead the people to create a happy life"; "People's desire for a good life is the objective of our struggle"; "Take benefiting the people as the greatest political achievement"; "The times we live in are the ones which set the examination papers, we officials are the ones who sit the exams, the people are the ones who mark the exam papers."

We should always bear in mind General Secretary Xi Jinping's instructions and apply a people-centric philosophy of development to all aspects of our reform and opening up, as well as social practice. We need to take people as our teachers and learn from them, be happy when they are happy and be worried when they suffer hardship, and forever share a common fate with the masses and link our hearts with the people's hearts. Let us hand in a satisfactory answer sheet and write a new chapter of happy life for the people.

## part two

# Running a Country is Rooted in Benefiting Ordinary People

1. Attaching importance to people's livelihood

2. Promoting virtue to the people

3. Enjoying great popularity

治国有常民为本

INTERPRETATION
IN PART 2 PROVIDED BY

-

**Professor Zhao Dongmei**
*Peking University*

&

**Professor Wang Jie**
*Central Party School*

# ONE
# ATTACHING IMPORTANCE TO PEOPLE'S LIVELIHOOD

" As the saying goes: '*Running a country is rooted in benefiting ordinary people.*' A people-centric philosophy of development is not an abstract or abstruse notion, therefore it must not remain in word only, or go no further than being an ideology, but reflect all aspects of socioeconomic development. We must uphold the belief that people are the main body of society and satisfy the people's aspirations for a good life, constantly realise, maintain and develop well the basic interests of the broad masses of the people, and achieve development that is for the people and depends on the people, ensuring that the people share the fruits of development."

— XI JINPING

THIS EXCERPT IS from a speech delivered by General Secretary Xi Jinping at a seminar for the main provincial-level leaders to study and implement the spirit of the 5th Plenum of the CPC's 18th National Congress, 18 January 2016.

### According to **Professor Zhao Dongmei:**

The adage "*Running a country is rooted in benefiting ordinary people*" comes from the *Huainanzi: A Compendium of Essays*. Its meaning is clear, simple and easy to understand. It says that the principle of governing a country is basically to benefit the people and let the common people enjoy real gains.

In the *Records of the Grand Historian* and the *Stratagems of the Warring States* both compiled in the West Han dynasty (206BC-25AD), when mentioning King Wuling of Zhao's reform of 'wearing barbarian uniform and the use of cavalry in battle', they said: "*The running of a state is always based on benefiting the people; the government decrees must be carried out without obstacles.*" Among all the states in China at the time, the Zhao State was close to the northern border, meaning its people lived together with nomadic tribesmen who lived on horseback. When at war, the tribesmen's cavalry was so flexible that the Zhao State's army constantly suffered losses. After repeated defeats, King Wuling decided to introduce horsemanship and archery to his army and developed his own cavalry.

Therefore, his army had to learn how to ride horses. When we talk about the issue today, we may feel that it is a very simple thing. But at the time it was indeed a very important technology import. The army uniform had to be changed, which was a tremendous cultural and psychological challenge for the ancient Chinese.

After a lot of hard thinking, King Wuling of Zhao was determined to adopt the ideology of '*running a country is rooted in benefiting ordinary people*'. Since cavalry and archery could protect the production and life of his people, things that could benefit his subjects, he had to surmount every difficulty to carry out the project. Therefore, King Wuling of Zhao's campaign of 'wearing barbarian uniform and the use of cavalry in battle' was carried out in spectacular fashion and the Zhao State reached the most powerful and prosperous stage in its history.

### According to **Professor Wang Jie:**

The adage "*running a country is rooted in benefiting ordinary people*" summarises several thousand years of China`s wisdom and experience of government officialdom and managing state affairs, as well as an important adaptation to present-day governance. These ideologies bequeathed to us by our ancestors are still of important significance to our practical work today.

For several decades General Secretary Xi Jinping has put most of his efforts and concern into the people's livelihood.

On 29 December 2012, two days before New Year's Day 2013, he travelled 480 kilometres by car to Fuping county in Hebei province to inspect work on poverty alleviation and development. On the same night he listened to a report from the main leaders of the provincial, municipal and county governments. Early the next morning, braving freezing temperatures, he visited several poverty-stricken villages. At the villagers' homes, he sat cross-legged on the *kang* (heatable brick or adobe bed) and asked them details about their annual income, whether they had enough winter clothes to wear, enough food to eat, enough charcoal to keep them warm, how far their children had to travel to school, and how difficult it was for them to see a doctor.

Afterwards he went to the office of the village committee and discussed how to help the villagers to end poverty with the village cadres, villagers and the village-based cadres from the higher-level organisations.

General Secretary Xi Jinping said: "Whether we can bring about a moderately prosperous society in all respects depends on how the people from villages live." This saying strategically points out the crux of building China into a moderately prosperous society in all respects. Poverty alleviation is the greatest project in contemporary China, and also the greatest project to benefit and enrich the people, so we must win this battle to allow those living in poverty and impoverished areas to enter the moderately prosperous society with all the other Chinese people.

## TWO
## PROMOTING VIRTUE TO THE PEOPLE

> When talking about cultivating virtue, one needs to have high ambitions as well as pragmatic plans. To devote oneself to one's country and to serve one's people, this is a great virtue. Those who cultivate great virtue can accomplish great undertakings. Meanwhile, one needs to start from doing small things well and be self-disciplined even in small matters, *'imitate what is good, and correct what is at fault'*. One needs to steadily cultivate public and personal virtue, and learn to work, be thrifty, be grateful, help others, be modest, be tolerant, examine oneself and practice self-restraint."

— XI JINPING

THIS EXCERPT IS from General Secretary Xi Jinping's speech at a seminar with teachers and students of Peking University, 4 May 2014.

### According to **Professor Zhao Dongmei:**

The maxim *"Imitate what is good, correct what is at fault,"* comes from the 42nd hexagram of the *Book of Changes*. The original text reads: *'If a superior man sees good, he imitates it, and corrects whatever faults he has."* This is about how to conduct oneself in society and cultivate one's moral character; or in today's words, how one can become a better person, or a better citizen. That is to say one must look at one's own weaknesses, compare them to the strong points of others, learn from them, and draw closer to these merits. This is what *"imitate what is good"* means. What should one do when one finds that one has done something wrong, or not well enough? One must correct it immediately. One must not be afraid to correct mistakes. Only by doing so can one make constant progress and become a gentleman, or in today's language a qualified, better citizen.

This adage has three levels of meaning.

First, one must forever maintain one's zeal for improvement, and never be complacent but make constant progress. No matter whether *"imitating what is good"* or *"correcting what is at fault"*, it is about making progress, making improvements and making oneself better.

Second, every one of us needs to take pains to undertake introspection. Confucianism advocates that *'introspection should be practiced on a daily basis'*. *'Introspection'* is self-examination. Only by constantly examining what one has done can one make constant progress.

Third, what attitude should one take when one perceives a better person or something better? One should think to emulate the virtuous. The most distinguished ancient scholars profoundly understood their learning. They turned what they had learned into action and influenced society. They were very good at introspection. They had the courage to correct their mistakes, were able to integrate knowledge with action and tempered themselves in practice thereby achieving continuous progress. Today we can turn our noses up at the ancients regarding science, technology, matter and knowledge, and we should act and be better than them in this respect. However in spirit, the progressive ways and means pointed out by the ancients are worth learning from, and such learning never goes out of date.

# THREE
## ENJOYING GREAT POPULARITY

“ There is an old saying: *'The water that keeps a boat afloat can also capsize it.'* This is something we must firmly keep in mind and never ever forget. The people are the sky above us and the earth below us. If we forget the people and become distanced from them, we will lose their support, like a stream with no source or a tree with no roots, and we will achieve nothing. Therefore, we must uphold the CPC's principle of relying on and serving the people, preserve our close ties with the people, readily subject ourselves to the criticism and oversight of the public, remain mindful of the difficulties ordinary people face, and search constantly for means of bringing people prosperity, so as to ensure that our Party always has the people's trust and support, and to ensure that our cause has an inexhaustible source of strength to carry it forward."

— XI JINPING

THIS EXCERPT IS from a speech of General Secretary Xi Jinping at the ceremony commemorating the 80th anniversary of the victory of the Long March, 21 October 2016.

### According to **Professor Zhao Dongmei:**

The allusion to *"The water that keeps a boat afloat can also capsize it"* first appeared in *Xunzi: Royal Regulations*. The original text reads: *"A ruler is a boat, while the common people are the water. The water keeps a boat afloat but also capsizes it."* In plain language it means that a monarch is like a boat, while the common people are like water; the water can support a boat and can also engulf it.

This metaphor of Xun Kuang (313-218BC) contains people-oriented thoughts, which is that people are important and they are the foundation of a kingdom. The relationship between the people and a monarch is likened to water and a boat, a vivid metaphor. From the changes of dynasties in history, again and again we see how water supported a boat and also sank it. For example, in the Sui dynasty (581-618AD) many things that had been done by Emperor Yang, when viewed many years later and from the perspective of history, or from the lofty perspective reached by an eagle, we can feel that they were positive, significant and valuable. But history cannot only be viewed from this sole perspective. When we view history, we cannot only stand at the height reached by an eagle or measure it using the yardstick of one or two thousand years. In fact, when we view history, the most important thing for us to see is how the people's lives were at the time. From this standpoint, we see that under the rule of Emperor Yang of Sui, the people lived a life of frequent wars and intensive labour. Such a life meant real suffering. The people had no way out. It was so outrageous that one by one, like drops of water, they constituted a giant indignant wave, which in the end overthrew the Sui court. The demise of the Sui dynasty illustrated how water supported a boat and upset it. In the Tang dynasty (618-907AD), because Emperor Taizong personally witnessed and experienced the demise of the Sui dynasty, the lessons of the downfall of the Sui court were still fresh in his mind, so he profoundly understood the truth of *"the water that keeps a boat afloat can also capsize it"*. He believed it so much that he was able to accept the criticisms of his ministers, which led to the evolution of the Benign Administration of the Zhenguan Reign Period which we all know today.

Regarding the Benign Administration of the Zhengguan Reign Period, I think the majority of us misunderstand it, feeling that during this period the Tang dynasty was very powerful and prosperous and its national strength had exceeded that of the Sui dynasty twenty years previously. But the fact was that when the Tang dynasty became powerful and prosperous it was a hundred years later in the 'Reign of Kaiyuan'. In the 'Reign of Zhengguan', no matter whether with regard to the population or the goods stockpiled in storehouses, it was far worse than in the latter years of the Sui dynasty. But why do we cherish such a memory and praise the 'Reign of Zhengguan'? And what did it actually look like in that period?

*The Political Program in Zhengguan Times* says that it was very safe in the streets and roads in those days. Travelling was safe and there were no muggers. The prisons were often empty as there were no offenders. Cattle and sheep grazed in the fields. When people left home, they did not need to lock their front doors. Due to bumper harvests for years running, grain was so cheap that one *dou* (about ten litres) only cost three or four copper coins. When going on a journey from the capital Chang'an to Linnan, or from Shandong to the sea, there was no need for travellers to take grain with them, because they could buy food and other items along the way. In Shandong, villagers treated guests and travellers cordially and even prepared dry provisions for them when they left. This was the Benign Administration of the Zhengguan Reign Period described by people in the Tang dynasty. As far as the national strength is concerned, it was not particularly solid at that time, or was even worse than in the latter years of the Sui dynasty, but society was harmonious, peaceful and happy. People living at the time were like peaceful seawater under a blue sky. They supported the giant ship of the Tang dynasty's forward motion. One or two civilians are insignificant, but when they gather together, they are the decisive power in the rise and fall of a regime.

## According to **Professor Wang Jie:**

Only by constantly improving people's livelihood can we enjoy great popularity. This is dialectics. So General Secretary Xi Jinping pointed out that we must take improving the well-being of the people and promoting people's overall development as the basis and starting point for development. That is to say we must truly work hard and act practically to win the hearts of the people. The people's recognition is the highest commendation and the people's trust is the greatest support to the government.

**part three**

# A Country Without Virtue Cannot Prosper

国无德不兴

INTERPRETATION
IN PART 3 PROVIDED BY

-

**Professor Yang Yu**
*Zhonqnan University*

&

**Professor Ai Silin**
*Tsinghua University*

# ONE
## WHY ESTABLISH VIRTUE?

" Each era has its spirit, as well as its values. Propriety, justice, integrity and honour are the four dimensions that maintain a state, *'when the four dimensions cannot be implemented, the state is sure to fall.'* This was our ancestors' understanding of their core values. What are the core values of our people and country today? This is both a theoretical and practical question. We have put forward that we must promote core socialist values. These values that we should cultivate and practice are prosperity, democracy, civility, harmony, freedom, equality, justice, the rule of law, patriotism, dedication, integrity and friendship. The values of prosperity, democracy, civility and harmony are for the country, those of freedom, equality, justice and the rule of law are for society; and those of patriotism, dedication, integrity and friendship are for citizens. They explain what type of country and society we are striving for, and what kind of citizens we are cultivating."

— XI JINPING

THIS EXCERPT IS from General Secretary Xi Jinping's speech at a symposium with teachers and students of Peking University, 4 May 2014.

### According to **Professor Yang Yu:**

General Secretary Xi Jinping here alludes to one of the famous classical adages: *"When the four dimensions cannot be implemented, the state is sure to fall."* This saying is from the ancient classic *Guanzi*. The original text reads: "The state has four dimensions (维 *wei*)... What are these four dimensions? The first one is propriety, the second one is righteousness, the third one is integrity, and the fourth one is a sense of shame." The original meaning of 'wei' was a string that tied things together, which extended to an object that all things depended on to be fastened. "A state has four dimensions" means that propriety, righteousness, integrity and a sense of shame are the social order and law for managing a state. If any one of the four is eliminated, the state will be in danger. If all four are eliminated, the state will be totally destroyed.

People may ask for a concrete explanation of the four dimensions, or the four cardinal virtues. "Propriety" is the legal code of conduct and moral standards that a group of people in a community should jointly observe. "Righteousness", simply speaking, is fairness, justice, which is the principle of ethics and also the foundation of integrity. In *Guanzi*, furthermore, "righteousness" also contained the meaning of declining out of modesty, that is to say, that we must restrain our individual desires or lust but give more opportunities to others. "Integrity" is justice, being incorruptible, not being extravagant, not being greedy, not covering up ugly and evil things, but being just and honest, fair and square. "A sense of shame", as the term suggests, means that people should have a sense of honour, and not tolerate evil.

"A state has four dimensions" says that each era has its values to pursue. Propriety, justice, integrity and honour are the values that an era generally pursues, and "if the four dimensions cannot be implemented, the state is sure to fall". Observe social norms, pursue fairness and justice, be aware of honour and do good deeds, these are fundamental safeguards for a country's prosperity and strength, and for a peaceful society.

TWO

## ESTABLISH WHAT KIND OF VIRTUE?

“ In the *Great Learning* chapter of the *Book of Rites*, it says: *'What the Great Learning teaches is to display illustrious virtue, to reinvigorate the people, and to rest in the highest excellence.'* At all times and in all countries, with regard to education and running a school, there have been various schools of thought and different theories and viewpoints, but the common understanding is that the aim of teaching must be for training and fostering what is needed for social development. Speaking in concrete terms, it is to nurture and educate those who are needed for social development, for accumulation of knowledge and cultural inheritance, for keeping a state going and its system of operation. Therefore, ancient and modern, Chinese and foreign, every country trains its talent according to its own political requirements. All the world's first-class universities have been developed during the process of serving the development of their own countries. Our country's socialist education is to train and foster the builders of socialism and their successors.”

— XI JINPING

THIS EXCERPT IS from General Secretary Xi Jinping's speech at a seminar with teachers and students of Peking University, 2 May 2018.

### According to **Professor Yang Yu:**

The maxim of *"What the Great Learning teaches is to display illustrious virtue, to reinvigorate the people, and to rest in the highest excellence"* is the basic creed of the chapter on *Great Learning* in the *Book of Rites*, or the highest state sought by "men of high moral character". "Illustrious virtue" means bright, fine virtue. The verb "display" means to bring out conspicuously. "To reinvigorate the people" means to promote this bright, fine virtue to the populace, getting rid of ignorance and developing people's intelligence, thereby reaching the highest state of moral cultivation, that is, *"to rest in the highest excellence"*.

Qu Yuan (340-278BC) was a patriotic Chinese poet who once took on the job of fostering young talent for his state. The official post granted to him shared some similarity with the function of our education ministry today. Don't we often compare teachers to hard-working gardeners and young students to flowers in a garden? This comparison was started by Qu Yuan. He once compared the young students he was teaching to flowers and grass, such as orchids, wild ginger, *angelica dahurica*, which grew in the Chu State, and himself to the gardener who worked hard to tend to them. His main aspiration was that they could grow healthy and strong, and when they grew into branches and leaves, he would then harvest them, turning them into people of tremendous talent for the state. Having people who possessed such integrity and ability to serve the state, why worry that the state could not have a bright future?

Zhou Dunyi (1017-1073AD), the neo-Confucianist of the Northern Song dynasty, said that *"(the lotus) grows out of the mud but remains unsoiled, cleansed by the pure water but not seductive"* in his classical work of prose *On Love of the Lotus*. Zhou Dunyi's philosophy of nurturing one's morals and self-cultivation descended in one continuous line from Qu Yuan's thought of fostering talent.

These two cases are about educating and fostering talent at national level. On the social or individual family level, I can use a classical story to illustrate the point.

When Su Shi (1037-1101AD) was a young boy, his mother Lady Cheng often taught him and his brother to read. One day, Lady Cheng was reading the history of the Eastern Han dynasty (25-220AD). Suddenly she could not help but heave a few deep sighs. Su Shi was standing by his mother's side, so he asked her whether she would be happy if he set his mind on becoming a man like Fan Pang. Lady Cheng closed the book and said: "If you can make up your mind to become a man like Fan Pang, how can I not be Fan Pang's mother?"

According to the record in the *Biography of Fan Pang* in the *Book of the Later Han*, Fan Pang was an honest and upright official who lived during the reign of Emperor Ling of Han. Politically it was an atrocious period when many honest scholars were butchered wantonly. In order not to drag others into trouble, Fan Pang decided to turn himself in to the authorities. When he bade farewell to his mother, he said that he had not been a filial son; although it was a worthy death about which he had nothing to regret, he regretted that he was no longer able to support and look after his mother. Lady Cheng said stoically that his choice was as popular as the choices of the truly celebrated scholars in history, a respectful deed; even if he were to die, what was there to regret?

So from the conversation between Fan Pang and his mother, we can deduce that the conversation between Su Shi and his mother not only expressed Su Shi's aspiration as a child, but also displayed his mother's moral courage and wisdom.

Therefore, the saying *"what the Great Learning teaches is to display illustrious virtue, to reinvigorate the people, and to rest in the highest excellence"* represents not only the highest realm of thought sought by ancient men of noble character, but the gentlemanly integrity and self-cultivation still called for by today's education and social conventions.

# THREE
## HOW TO CULTIVATE VIRTUE?

> Since ancient times the Chinese have stressed *'studying the nature of things to acquire knowledge, correcting thoughts with sincerity, cultivating one's moral character, managing the family, governing the state and safeguarding peace under Heaven'*. As we see it today the principles of *'studying the nature of things to acquire knowledge, correcting thoughts with sincerity and cultivating one's moral character'* are for individuals; the principle of *'managing the family'* is for society; and those of *'governing the state and safeguarding peace under Heaven'* are for the country. The core socialist values we have put forward are a combination of requirements for the country, society and citizens, which represent the nature of socialism, carry forward outstanding traditional Chinese culture, draw on the best of world civilisation and reflect the spirit of the times".

— XI JINPING

THIS EXCERPT IS from General Secretary Xi Jinping's speech at a seminar with teachers and students of Peking University, 4 May 2014.

### According to **Professor Yang Yu,**
just as with the previous quote:

*"What the Great Learning teaches is to display illustrious virtue, to reinvigorate the people, and to rest in the highest excellence"*, the quote in this paragraph is also from Confucius' *Great Learning*. The original text is quite long, but the quote in this paragraph is succinct.

If *"what the Great Learning teaches is to display illustrious virtue, to reinvigorate the people, and to rest in the highest excellence"* is about the highest state of moral cultivation and the three cardinal guides of the *Great Learning*, then *"studying the nature of things to acquire knowledge, correcting thoughts with sincerity, cultivating one's moral character, managing the family, governing the state and safeguarding peace under Heaven"* are the eight specific ways, the so-called 'Eight Items' of realising the three cardinal guides.

We can see that the practice of the 'Eight Items' seems a long and arduous process, and in fact that is really the case.

Let me use Fan Zhongyan (989-1052AD), the famous chancellor in the Northern Song dynasty, as an example to illustrate the point. In his five years' study in the Yingtian Institute, Fan Zhongyan was the most diligent and painstaking student among his peers. When he was twenty-seven years old, he passed the highest imperial examination to become an official. The first thing he did after he became an official was to bring his mother to his mansion so he could look after her. By 1040, Fan Zhongyan was over fifty years old, but he undertook a dangerous mission, being transferred from the rich and beautiful south of the Yangtze River to the western border region where the weather was cold and living conditions were tough. During the time when he was stationed in Qingzhou to defend the border, he wrote his famous verse *Yujia'ao*, a poetic masterpiece through the ages, in which he expressed his ardent zeal to dedicate himself to subduing the invading enemy and to serving his country. In fact, only after we understand his lyrics *"Be the first to bear the world's hardships, and the last to enjoy its comforts"*, the core spirit of his poem *'Memorial to Yueyang Tower"*, can we understand his *"Grey is my hair, the warrior is in tears"* in the *Yujia'ao*. Fan Zhongyan did not shed tears of frustration worrying about his own future and destiny, but he shed tears of kindheartedness and felt concern for the destiny of the people under Heaven.

A renowned chancellor in the Northern Song dynasty, Fan Zhongyan was a statesman, military commander and man of letters. After he died, Emperor Renzong offered him the title 'Duke of Wenzheng'.

The word *Wen* was the highest plaudit given to the learning of a man in the Song dynasty, while the word *Zheng* was the highest plaudit the public could give a man for his moral cultivation. I feel that Fan Zhongyan's life experience was an example to illustrate how we should complete our knowledge, be sincere in our thoughts, rectify our hearts, cultivate our morals, regulate our families, rightly govern the state, and make the country tranquil and happy. Today it still possesses an important guiding significance to the cultivation of people's character and the development of their competence.

### According to **Professor Ai Silin:**

Regarding moral cultivation, I have a few points to make.

First, study diligently. It is the basic way to cultivate one's moral character. But how to achieve it? Everyone has their own understanding. My view is that we must learn from the moral models around us.

I would like to talk about an ethical model, whom General Secretary Xi Jinping has received twice and affectionately called her 'Auntie'. She is Gong Quanzhen, the widow of General Gan Zuchang, a founding general of the People's Republic. In 1957 she returned with her husband to the countryside and became a farmer. In the last few decades, she did not concern herself about pay but gave the local people lectures about revolutionary tradition, moral values and faith. She was very thrifty, never willing to buy herself new clothes, but readily took out the majority of her income to aid needy students, old people with no heirs and no family support, and neighbours who needed help. She is over ninety years old, but is still concerned about society and helping others.

To study diligently we must learn from our fine traditional culture, which is the root of the Chinese nation. We must not abandon it, otherwise we will be a nation with no roots.

Second, make a clear distinction between right and wrong, good and evil, beauty and ugliness, and make good choices. General Secretary

Xi Jinping has said that the young face a wide range of choices. But what is important for the young is to be guided by a correct world view, outlook on life and sense of values when they are making choices. Once they have a correct world view, outlook on life and sense of values, they hold the key.

Third, be honest and sincere. Moral cultivation cannot be empty talk but must be put into practice. I think moral cultivation should start from childhood. General Secretary Xi Jinping has said that his understanding of the word 'people' came from his experience in northern Shaanxi when he was a 16 or 17-year-old school graduate who went to live and work in a production team. So he would often say that the young must learn how to conduct themselves, to think every day about whether I am a patriot? Or do I love the collective? Or do I treat my parents with filial respect at home? Or do I take good care of my classmates? Or have I complied with public morality? Do it every day. The accumulation of every bit can help you cultivate a great moral character.

The cultivation of virtue cannot be done in a single day. It is the outcome of a gradual accumulation over days and months. "Do not do evil things though they may be insignificant; do not give up good things though they may be minor." Why? Because "the accumulation of good deeds is sufficient to make one famous; the accumulation of evil deeds is sufficient to destroy one's life." General Secretary Xi Jinping has alluded to these adages on many occasions to warn Party members and cadres that they should do more small acts of goodness but refrain from even small deeds of evil.

The important thing for cultivating virtue is perseverance. Comrade Mao Zedong said: "It is not difficult for one to do some good deeds. What's difficult is to do good deeds all one's life and never do anything evil." If we want to be a person of noble moral character, we must always bear in mind that moral cultivation is a perpetual process, and always starts from now, and from oneself.

# part four
# Families are the Basis of a Country

1. Attach great importance to the family household

2. Attach great importance to family education

3. Attach great importance to family traditions

国之本在家

INTERPRETATION
IN PART 4 PROVIDED BY

-

**Professor Zhao Dongmei**
*Peking University*

&

**Professor Wang Jie**
*Central Party School*

# ONE
## ATTACH GREAT IMPORTANCE TO THE FAMILY HOUSEHOLD

> The Chinese nation has always attached great importance to family households, just like the old saying goes: '*Kingdoms are the basis of the empire, families are the basis of a kingdom*'. Family harmony leads to prosperity in all undertakings. As China becomes prosperous and strong, and China realises its national rejuvenation, this is eventually reflected in the happiness of millions of families and the constant improvement of billions of people's lives. Only when every family is happy can the country flourish and the nation thrive."

> — XI JINPING

THIS EXCERPT IS from General Secretary Xi Jinping's greetings to the Chinese people at the 2018 Spring Festival Greeting Party.

### According to **Professor Zhao Dongmei:**

The saying "*Kingdoms are the basis of the empire, families are the basis of a kingdom*" comes from *Mencius*. The ancient philosopher Mencius said: "People have this common saying: 'The kingdom, the state, the family.' The root of the kingdom is the state. The root of the state is the family. The root of the family is the person at its head." It means that the root of the kingdom, the state and the family lies in each individual household, and the root of each household lies in each individual person. Every individual person should seriously try their best to be a good person and be the best version of themselves, after that they can build a harmonious and happy family. When family households are harmonious and happy, the state can be in good order and the country can be at peace.

This is a full, practical programme of how to build a happy society. From the world, the state and the household to the individual person, the core is the household, not the individual person. Because, after all, each individual is the result of family education, or family education of self-restraint.

Here I want to tell an ancient story. We should all have heard the story of Sima Guang breaking the vat. How little hero Sima Guang calmly, bravely broke the water vat and saved his playmate, a story told from the Song dynasty until today. But from the written records left by Sima Guang himself, we have never read anything about this heroic deed of his. In his own account and memory, what was the most important and impressive thing in his childhood? It was a story about a green walnut.

At the time Sima Guang was only five or six years old. He had an elder sister who was much older than him. One day, when they were playing together, they tried to remove the outer green husk of a walnut. We know it is a very difficult thing to do. The sister and brother tried for half a day but to no avail. Discouraged, the sister left and went to do something else, leaving Sima Guang to carry on trying his luck. Then an aged servant came along. Experienced, the servant went to bring some hot water and soaked the green walnut in it for a while then removed the green husk from the walnut. The servant walked away, leaving Sima Guang to play with the walnut. When the sister returned, she asked Sima Guang who had removed the green husk. Raising his head, Sima Guang said proudly that he had done it. Then his father's expression became grave and he said: "I was watching you all the time. How can you tell lies, little child?" Because his father had shouted at him, telling him that little children must not tell lies, it left a deep impression on Sima Guang.

Many years later Sima Guang mentioned this in a letter, saying that ever since then he could never dare to tell lies or boast. Telling no lies and being honest was the teaching Sima Guang learned from his father. After Sima Guang grew into an adult, he had a deeper understanding of the word 'honest'. He had once said that honesty had to come from one's inner heart because if you are honest, what you express is accepted by others. Being honest and treating others with sincerity, not hiding one's own feelings, bravely expressing one's own opinions, holding firmly to the truth and adhering to principles were to become life-long principles of Sima Guang's social conduct.

Later, when one of his students was leaving, he asked Sima Guang to write him a motto. Sima Guang had a think, then he told the student that if he truly wanted a motto, he would present him with the word 'honest'. The student asked how he could manage to be honest. Sima Guang said that he could start by not telling lies. Sima Guang practiced this virtue all his life and he did indeed practice what he preached; meanwhile he passed this beautiful seed on to his student, the seed sowed in Sima Guang's heart when his father shouted at him that time.

A good family tradition breeds good people, as well as good seeds. When people bring this seed to a wider field to influence more people, they create a more harmonious and better social atmosphere. And this is "*The root of the kingdom is the state. The root of the state is the family. The root of the family is the person at its head*".

## According to **Professor Wang Jie:**

Where there is family, there is family tradition. Harmony in the family leads to prosperity in all undertakings. Only when every family is happy, can the state flourish and the country thrive. Regarding attaching importance to family development, General Secretary Xi Jinping has talked about two aspects. First, the future and destiny of families are closely linked to the future and destiny of the country and the nation. That is to say we must not only be concerned about our own small family, but also be concerned about the state, the big family. Since time immemorial, there have been many examples and models that are worth learning from and respecting. Looking at our history, we see that countless ancient sages upheld the conviction that "a country is in good order once family households are managed well, while cultivating one's moral character starts from correcting oneself", and cherished the sentiment of "upholding the interests of the country with one's life regardless of what may befall one". They conscientiously and closely integrated the destiny of the individual and the family with the destiny of the country and the nation, writing a succession of touching and inspiring stories for us.

During the revolutionary war years, on the land of China where it was thick with gunpowder fumes and destruction could be seen everywhere, heroic and moving stories like "mothers encouraging their sons to fight the Japanese invaders and wives sending their husbands to the fields of battle" emerged in great numbers. Civilians made their last piece of cloth into army uniforms, donated their last morsel of food as military rations, their last door panel as a stretcher, and sent their last son to the battlefield. This was an exquisite demonstration of the patriotic sentiment of protecting our homes and defending our country, and of everyone alive fulfilling their duty to their country.

Second, blend the realisation of family dreams with the national dream.

The Chinese Dream is not an unattainable concept that has nothing to do with us, nor too high a goal, nor a mirage. It is around us and in the heart of every one of us. Only after the great rejuvenation of the Chinese nation is realised, can the dream of each family be realised and come true. When every family is happy, the country flourishes and the nation thrives. Therefore, among millions of families, we must conscientiously connect loving our family to loving our country, integrating our family dream with the great dream of rejuvenating China. We must think and work with one heart and one mind, gathering the wisdom and zeal of the 400 million Chinese families and 1.3 billion Chinese people, turning them into a majestic strength to realise the Two Centenary Goals and the great rejuvenation of the Chinese nation.

NOTE:

*The Two Centenary Goals were put forward at the 18th CPC National Congress. By 2021, with the 100th anniversary of the CPC, China will become a moderately prosperous country in all aspects; by 2049, with the 100th anniversary of the founding of New China (the PRC), China will become a prosperous, strong, democratic, civilised, harmonious, socialist, modern society.*

TWO

## ATTACH GREAT IMPORTANCE TO FAMILY EDUCATION

" The ancients said: '*When you love your son, you should teach him righteous ways*', and '*If you love your son in the wrong way, such love only does him harm*'. Young boys and girls are the future and hope of families, as well as the country. The ancients knew that to feed without teaching is the father's fault, so families should take on the responsibility of teaching the younger generation. Guardians, particularly parents, have a great influence on their children, and this influence often affects them for the rest of their life."

— XI JINPING

THIS EXCERPT IS from General Secretary Xi Jinping's speech when he received representatives of the winners of the First National Civilised Families Vote, 12 December 2016.

### According to **Professor Zhao Dongmei:**

The saying "*When you love your son, you should teach him righteous ways*" comes from *The Commentary of Zuo (Zuo Zhuan)*, while "*If you love your son in the wrong way, such love can only do him harm*" originates from *The Comprehensive Mirror to Aid in Government (Zizhi Tongjian)*.

We know that from *Zuo Zhuan* to *Zizhi Tongjian*, there was an interval of 1,500 years. But the two sayings speak about the same thing either positively or negatively, which is how we should love our children and what kind of parental love really benefits children. Behind these two sentences are hidden two human tragedies.

In *Zuo Zhuan*, the man who said "*When you love your son, you should teach him righteous ways*" was Shi Que, a cabinet minister to Duke

Zhuang of the Wei State in the Spring and Autumn Period (770-476BC). Why did Shi Que say this? Because he saw Duke Zhuang of Wei loving his youngest son Zhouyu in a way that went against moral principles. Fond of the military and weaponry, Zhouyu liked to brandish spears and sticks, so he was surrounded by a large bunch of desperadoes. Anyone with any sense could see that if Zhouyu was allowed to carry on like this, he might be haughty because he was his father's favourite, which would threaten the position of the crown prince and consequently destabilise the political situation in Wei State. Therefore, the courageous old minister Shi Que took a stand by telling Duke Zhuang: "*When you love your son, you should teach him righteous ways.*" He even said to Duke Zhuang that if he really wanted to depose his eldest son and appoint his youngest son as the crown prince, he had to hurry up and settle the matter. If he left the matter unsettled, he would harm the state and bring disaster on it. But this Duke Zhuang was a very timid man. He dared not depose his eldest son and appoint his youngest son as the crown prince, which would have openly violated etiquette, so he went on loving Zhouyu carelessly.

We can see that Duke Zhuang's love for his son was a very timid love and he went on tolerating Zhouyu's development of his force. What were the consequences? After Duke Zhuang died, the crown prince ascended the throne, but he was soon killed by Zhouyu. Could Zhouyu have been a care-free king of Wei State? He was killed by his subjects. Neither of Duke Zhuang's sons had a good death. After all, it was Duke Zhuang's wrong love in contravention of moral principles that killed them.

However, what gives us much food for thought is that the muddleheaded father Duke Zhuang seemed not to be the only one, hence the saying: "*If you love your son in the wrong way, such love can only do him harm*". Who was this muddleheaded father? He was Shi Hu, the ruler of Later Zhao (319-352 AD) during the Sixteen States Period (304-439 AD). Shi Hu had a crown prince called Shi Xuan, but he loved his younger son Shi Tao more, so the father gave the crown prince Shi Xuan and the younger son Shi Tao equal opportunities, letting them take turns to deal with national affairs. He himself became a hands-off monarch, only too glad to have the chance to live an idle life. But his decision made his minister Shen Zhong uneasy and anxious, so Shen Zhong said to Shi Hu: "*If you love your son in the wrong way, such love can only do him harm.*" It means that if you don't use moral principles to love your sons, your love will do them harm. The result was that Shi Xuan killed Shi Tao, then Shi Hu killed Shi Xuan. For human beings, nothing is more tragic than an elder brother killing his younger brother and a father killing his son.

Why did tragedies resulting from the wrong love of parents happen again and again? Because to pamper one's children is easy, but to "*teach your children righteous ways*" is very difficult. Because first the parents must distinguish what is right and what are '*righteous ways*', then they must use their brains to analyse and make efforts to learn. Parents must be clear about what is good for their children, so they must acquire knowledge, use their brains to think and understand that '*if you love your son in the wrong way, such love can only bring him harm*', study hard the way to '*teach your children righteous ways*' and give your children the right sort of love.

## According to **Professor Wang Jie:**

General Secretary Xi Jinping has spoken about three aspects of family education.

First, he said: "*The family is life's first classroom, while parents are children's first teachers.*" Family education governs how children are brought up. Therefore, parents must pass on good moral character and habits to their children, giving them correct guidance to establish a correct world view, outlook on life and sense of values. From when they learn to speak and walk, children are educated and nurtured by their families, and are subconsciously influenced by what they see and hear from their parents. The *Three-Character Classic* said: "*Jade that has not been polished cannot be used. A person who has not studied cannot know righteousness.*" In the family, parents should be an example and model to their children. They must teach by example as well as by verbal instructions, practice what they preach, and educate their children well, thereby correctly buttoning the first button for their children and making their children take the correct first step in life.

Second, parents must take on the responsibility of educating their children. As parents, they must educate their children. As the saying goes: "*To feed without teaching is the father's fault.*" In our traditional culture and throughout Chinese history, there have been many examples of parents practicing strict family education, such as the stories we know very well: "Mencius' mother moved house three times to better her son's education", "Tao Kan's mother returned the fish sent to her by Tao Kan", "Yue Fei's mother tattooed 'Serve Your Country with Utmost Loyalty' on his back", and "Ouyang Xiu's mother taught him calligraphy by using a reed stalk on sand". All these are examples of the strict family education of our forefathers. That's what the old saying "*Where there is a strict father, there is a dutiful son*" means.

Third, family education involves many aspects, but the most important is education regarding moral character. Therefore, all parents should pass on good moral character and positive energy to their children. Fine family traditions are passed down from generation to generation, which silently influence their descendants.

# THREE
## ATTACH GREAT IMPORTANCE TO FAMILY TRADITIONS

"Family tradition is an important part of the social ethos. A family is not only a place where people live, but also a place for the soul to rest. A good family tradition brings prosperity and harmony to a family, while bad family traditions inevitably harm future generations and society. As an old saying goes: *'The family that accumulates goodness is sure to have an overabundance of happiness, and the family that accumulates evil is sure to have an overabundance of misery.'* Zhuge Liang's letter of admonishment to his son, the house instructions of Master Yan, and Mr Zhu Bolu's family motto, all promote some kind of family tradition. The revolutionaries of the elder generation, such as Mao Zedong, Zhou Enlai and Zhu De, all attached great importance to family tradition."

— XI JINPING

THIS EXCERPT IS from General Secretary Xi Jinping's speech when he received representatives of the winners of the First National Civilised Families Vote, 12 December 2016.

### According to **Professor Zhao Dongmei:**

The adage "*The family that accumulates goodness is sure to have an overabundance of happiness, and the family that accumulates evil is sure to have an overabundance of misery*" comes from the *Book of Changes*. Its meaning is very easy to understand. Families that often do good deeds will definitely have good luck and be happy, while households that often do evil will certainly suffer disaster. The key word is '*accumulate*'. Speaking in today's language, it is quantitative change that facilitates qualitative change.

What exactly is an 'overabundance of happiness'? This is a question we must think about deeply. In major terms, families foster people of great ability for the state; while generally in ordinary households, an 'overabundance of happiness' is due to harmony nourished by a family, which ensures children grow up healthily and the elderly get to live peacefully in their old age. This is what "the family that accumulates goodness is sure to have an overabundance of happiness" means.

Then what does an 'overabundance of misery' mean? Generally, tragedies that occurred in history are not small in number. Patricide and regicide, family members in discord, enmity between father and son, or brothers quarrelling at home, or family break ups. When it comes down to it, small problems accumulate in a family, which can make every family member feel unhappy, so they may live their lives in misery. We all know how valuable life is. Family education is subconscious, but it is also the most basic and solid preparation for every individual's life. Honest, kind-hearted parents with lofty ideals can foster children who are eager to make progress. Parents who are greedy, lazy and used to acting in a slipshod way have no reason to blame their children for being short of gumption. The value of family tradition can never be overemphasised.

# part five

# Grass Can't Repay the Sun's Warm Kindness

1. Respect the aged and love one's parents

2. Honour one's elders

报得三春晖

INTERPRETATION
IN PART 5 PROVIDED BY

-

**Professor Yang Yu**
*Zhongnan University*

&

**Professor Wang Jie**
*Central Party School*

# ONE
## RESPECT THE AGED AND LOVE ONE'S PARENTS

" Since ancient times the Chinese nation has attached great importance to the family as well as to affection between family members. Sayings like 'harmony in the family leads to prosperity in all undertakings', 'the happiness of a family reunion', 'respect the aged and love the young', 'dutiful wife and loving mother', 'help one's husband and bring up one's children', 'be industrious and thrifty in managing a household', all reflect this notion of the Chinese people. *'The threads in a kind mother's hand, a gown for her son bound for far-off lands. Sewn stitch by stitch before he leaves, for fear his return may be delayed. The kindness young grass receives from the warm sun can't be repaid.'* This verse from the *Song of a Roamer,* composed by the poet Meng Jiao in the Tang dynasty, vividly expresses such a deep family complex of the Chinese people."

— XI JINPING

THIS EXCERPT IS from General Secretary Xi Jinping's greetings to the Chinese people at the 2015 Spring Festival Greeting Party.

### According to **Professor Yang Yu:**

The author of the *'Song of a Roamer'* was a famous poet called Meng Jiao who lived in the middle Tang dynasty. Despite being talented, Meng Jiao failed in the imperial examination for half of his life until he was forty-six years old when he succeeded at metropolitan level and received the *Jinshi* degree. We know that in the Tang dynasty not every holder of the *Jinshi* degree could become an official immediately. They had to go through examinations organised by the court's personnel department; furthermore, whether a vacancy was available, or whether a candidate was recommended by a prominent person, were also prerequisites for them to become an official. After Meng Jiao received his *Jinshi* degree at the age of forty-six, he had no opportunity to enter officialdom until four years later when he was fifty years old. He finally received a letter of appointment to be a county official in Liyang. Although not very satisfactory, Meng Jiao at least had a position enabling him to settle down and get on with his life; besides that he had an income, the government salary was just enough for him to support his family. Therefore, after he arrived in Liyang County, the first thing he wanted to do was to go back home at once to bring his mother to Liyang, where he would support and look after her. He wrote the '*Song of a Roamer*' after a long separation from his mother and finally he was able to bring her to his place and to be with her for years to come.

I am sure when he wore the clothes sewn by his mother, no matter how far and how long he wandered from home, as soon as he thought of home and his mother waiting for him to come home, that put his mind at ease. If sewing clothes for a son about to embark on a long journey is a simple expression of every mother's love, then a son's profound feelings for his mother's love and his return to her love is more difficult to come by and more valuable. Therefore I think the heart of the poem does not lie in the first four lines but the last two: "*The kindness young grass receives from the warm sun can't be repaid.*"

To Meng Jiao, I feel that the word "*repaid*" in the verse is even more valuable. He failed the imperial examination at the metropolitan level until he was forty-six years old and obtained an official post of some kind when he was fifty years old, enabling him to accompany his mother for a relatively long time. I think if it were not for his mother's constant support and encouragement, he might have long since given up. Therefore, in my opinion, the last two lines also embody Meng Jiao's conscience-stricken feelings for his mother.

But of course, to every mother, it is not important how senior her son's official post is, or how much money he makes. What is important is his company. So it is not important how their children show their gratitude, but whether they intend to do so.

According to **Professor Wang Jie:**

In the culture of Confucianism, when it comes to treating one's parents with filial respect, it is not just about meeting their material needs. Therefore, Confucius said: "Nowadays filial piety means being able to feed your parents. But everyone does this even for horses and dogs. Without respect, what is the difference?" It means that meeting your parents' material needs is petty filial piety. Consequently, Zengzi said: "There are three degrees of filial piety. The highest is to honour your parents; the second is not to disgrace them; and the lowest is to be able to support them." As for how to treat one's parents with filial respect, the ancients were like us today. There are many different ways, so it is impossible to follow the same pattern, or have only one mode.

TWO
## HONOUR ONE'S ELDERS

> The Chinese nation has many traditional virtues, such as: respect the aged and love the young; the wife is virtuous at home so the husband can keep his mind on his work outside; the mother is kind and the son displays filial piety; the elder brother is amicable and the younger brother is respectful; do farm work while studying to bequeathe to the family; manage one's household industriously and thriftily; be well educated and exercise good judgement; observe the law and discipline; harmony in the family leads to prosperity in everything one does. Such virtues are ingrained in the mind and blended into the blood of the Chinese people, constituting an important moral strength supporting the Chinese nation's continuous development. They are a valuable source of intellectual wealth for the construction of family civilisation."

— XI JINPING

THIS EXCERPT IS from General Secretary Xi Jinping's speech when he received representatives of the winners of the First National Civilised Families Vote, 12 December 2016.

### According to **Professor Yang Yu:**

Respecting one's elders is indeed a fine traditional virtue of the Chinese nation. As early as in the Warring States Period (475-221BC), Mencius said: "If one loves one's parents and respects one's elders, the world will be at peace." It means that two thousand years ago, Mencius realised that honouring the aged was not only a matter of concern for one family, but for every family and every person in society.

Of course, on the one hand, honouring one's elders is a social responsibility, so the system, the nursing facilities and the social ethos must be perfected to ensure that the elderly are being looked after. On the other hand, it comes down to every one of us, and how each individual treats every elderly person beside us.

Why every elderly person beside us? I think this concept includes at least three layers of meaning.

First, our close kin, including our parents and grandparents with whom we are directly related by blood.

Second, those within the radius of our living circle. For example, elderly people who live in the same neighbourhood or the same community who need help.

Third, elderly people who are strangers with whom we are not directly associated. For instance, we can regularly or occasionally do what we can for elderly people on buses, underground trains, when crossing the road or in nursing homes.

If we can treat every elderly person around us as suggested by the *Students' Rules*: "Love everyone and become close with the kind-hearted", and as Mencius said: "Love one's parents and respect one's elders", our society will certainly be brimming over with kindheartedness and love.

This calls to mind a story which left a deep impression on me. The leading role was played by a famous man of letters, writer Li Mi in the Three Kingdom Period (224-287AD). Li Mi was originally an official of the Shu Han Kingdom. After Shu Han became extinct, the founder of the West Jin, Emperor Wu (Sima Yan) heard about Li Mi's talent and virtuousness, so he issued an edict appointing Li Mi to serve in his court. But Li Mi rejected it. How could he have refused an offer from an emperor? He explained his reasons in his famous *Memorial to the Emperor Expressing My Feelings,* which made his name go down in history. It turned out that Li Mi's father had died when Li Mi was very young. His mother remarried, so he was brought up by his grandmother Lady Liu. We know that from the Three Kingdom

Period to the Wei and Jin dynasties was a time when society was extremely unstable. So we can imagine how difficult it was for an old widow to look after a young child and bring him up.

When Li Mi wrote his *Memorial to the Emperor Expressing My Feelings*, his grandmother Lady Liu was ninety-six years old, while he himself was forty-four, in the prime of life. So he said to Emperor Wu of Jin that he had plenty of time to serve His Majesty, but the days he could be with his grandmother were numbered. "I have more days to serve Your Majesty, but less days to repay my grandmother. Out of my filial piety to serve and respect my relatives, I beg permission to look after my grandmother until her death." Then from the bottom of his heart he continued: "If it were not for my grandmother, I might not be alive today; but without me, it will be difficult for her to get through her remaining years." Even a baby crow knows to feed his old mother when it grows up, how can a human abandon his loved ones?

This *Memorial to the Emperor Expressing My Feelings* was very touching. It is said that after Emperor Wu of Jin read it, he was so moved by Li Mi's sincere spirit of filial piety that he did not force Li Mi to take up the official post, but granted him two maidservants to help look after Lady Liu, and also urged local officials to give Lady Liu some subsidies.

About a year after Li Mi wrote his *Memorial to the Emperor Expressing My Feelings*, his grandmother died. He then observed three years of mourning for his deceased grandmother. After three years of mourning, he finally agreed to the emperor's summons and became the crown prince's secretary. Li Mi's *Memorial to the Emperor Expressing My Feelings* became one of the most famous scripts of all time concerning filial piety and honouring the elderly, and a masterpiece handed down to later generations.

Li Mi's story of filial piety reminds me of another famous historical anecdote regarding honouring the elderly. It was about a man keeping rice crusts for his mother, a story included in *A New Account of Tales of the World*. There was a man called Chen Yi, whose mother had a special hobby. She liked very much to eat rice crusts. So when Chen Yi was on official business, when rice was cooked, he would always keep the crust and put it in a pouch for his mother to eat when he got home. Later, the pirate Sun En started a coup. At this moment Chen Yi had accumulated several *dou* (a unit of dry measure for grain, equivalent to ten litres) of rice crusts in the pouch. Before he could take them to his mother, he followed the troops and rushed to the front line. They were defeated. The troops were broken up and the soldiers fled into the mountains. Many of them died of starvation, but because Chen Yi was carrying the rice crusts with him, he survived. Everyone said that this was the best return for his filial piety to his mother.

This story was recorded in *A New Account of Tales of the World*, showing that even in the Wei and Jin dynasties when individual freedom was most valued, filial piety was still a highly praised virtue prevalent far and wide in society.

We can absolutely extend this genuine feeling of ours toward honouring the elderly to others, forming a good social atmosphere and creating its own virtuous cycle. Throughout history there were many stories like those of Li Mi and Chen Yi. Every time I read Du Fu's verses *"I'm happy to drink with my venerable neighbour, toasting the last cups across a bamboo fence"*, I am touched by how joyously the poet and his aged neighbour get along. When I read his line *"They gladly greet their father's bosom friend"*, I am always moved by the children's filial sentiments because such children not only treat their parents well, but are also considerate to their parents' friends. When I read the verses *"The children I meet on the way don't know me, 'Where do you come from, dear sir?' they smile and say"*, I always smilingly acknowledge the children's kindness to an old visitor.

As said in the *Book of Filial Piety*: "Of all creatures with their different natures produced by Heaven and Earth, man is the noblest. Of all the actions of man there is none greater than filial piety." There is no need to turn the classical language into the vernacular, we can all understand what it means. Because it expresses the traditional virtue of the Chinese in honouring the aged, and such a virtue has not disappeared today.

Every one of us gets old, so treating all the elderly around us well is within our capacity to achieve.

# part six
# Let the Universe be Full of Integrity

只留清气满乾坤

INTERPRETATION
IN PART **6** PROVIDED BY

-

**Professor Wang Liqun**
*Henan University*

&

**Professor Guo Jianning**
*Deputy Director of the Research Centre for the Theoretical System
of Socialism with Chinese Characteristics, Peking University*

# ONE
# WHAT IS THE CULTIVATION OF MORAL CHARACTER?

> Just like the poem says: '*Plum blossoms don't care about praise for their nice colour, they only want to leave a delicate fragrance lingering in the universe.*'
>
> There are many ways and means for Party members and officials to enhance our moral cultivation. The most important one is to conscientiously draw nutrients from China's fine traditional culture. We should learn honestly from the masses and always emulate those better than ourselves in all matters, use high standards to strengthen self-discipline and accept heteronomy."

— XI JINPING

THE MAXIM of *"emulating those better than oneself in all matters"* has been alluded to by General Secretary Xi Jinping on multiple occasions.

### According to **Professor Wang Liqun:**

We must all be familiar with this adage alluded to by General Secretary Xi Jinping. Confucius said in the chapter *Li Ren* of *The Analects of Confucius*: "*When seeing men of worth, we should think of equaling them; when seeing men of a contrary character, we should turn inward and examine ourselves.*"

This is about moral cultivation. It emphasises that the important criteria in moral cultivation are to follow the example of those who are virtuous and learn from them. Then what should we do when we see someone who is not so good? We should conduct self-examination to see if we have the same problem. So, when we see a good person, we should think about being like them; when we see someone not so good, we should reflect on our own weak points. This is a very important link when cultivating our moral character.

Let me use an example to illustrate this point. It happened in the fifth year of Emperor Jiajing's reign in the Ming dynasty, in Runing, which is now Runan County in Henan Province. The geographic location of the county was very important, meaning it was a vital regional communication link. The Ministry of Official Personnel Affairs appointed an official called Wang Ruxue to serve as the prefect of Runing. As soon as this appointment was issued, the public was very happy with it, saying it was an appropriate appointment. But some people were worried because the court had a regulation. Anyone who did a good job was promoted, and vice versa. Wang Ruxue was a capable official, so he was sure to be promoted and then leave the county. A scholar called He Tang wrote an article saying that people should not worry. As long as every official thinks of equaling those of worth, how can we predict that the new prefect will be inferior to Prefect Wang Ruxue? So the people in Runing worried no more, and welcomed any new prefects who came to promote the locals' well-being.

This is a well-known, as well as an ordinary story, which shows that the notion of *"When we see men of worth, we should think of equaling them"* has struck a deep chord in people's hearts.

### According to **Professor Guo Jianning:**

What is the cultivation of one's moral character? Why did General Secretary Xi Jinping stress the importance of it? Why must we be strict with our moral cultivation?

On 10 March 2018, in the first session of the 13th National Congress General Secretary Xi Jinping attended a group discussion of the Chongqing delegation. He pointed out that political ecology is the same as natural ecology. It is polluted by the slightest ignorance. If it goes wrong, the price is high if we want to recover from the error. This reminds me of a verse by Wang Yangming (1472-1529AD):

*"Everyone has intuitive knowledge, and the change of all things on earth lies in one's heart."* The *"heart"* here is conscience, intuitive knowledge, and also moral quality and character. Cultivating the Party spirit and upholding its ideals and convictions are the philosophical mindset of today's communists, as well as their foundation and cornerstone. Without them, we will be weak-willed and lose our bearings. We will get lost and lose our conscience which may well even result in academic misconduct and lack of sincerity. To conduct ourselves we must first cultivate our moral integrity and take it as the most essential virtue, the first step of our life.

Strictly cultivating moral character is a mandatory lesson for us to make an all-out effort to enforce strict Party discipline. Ever since the 18th CPC National Congress, we have had a series of new ideas, methods and measures on the issue, such as combating 'tigers' as well as 'flies' (that is, bringing corrupt officials to justice regardless of rank). The policy covers all areas, sectors and departments. The Party is applying zero tolerance to corruption leaving no stone unturned and sending out inspection groups. To accomplish all this, the first step is to cultivate ourselves. Speaking about its significance, self-cultivation is not only a mandatory lesson but the first subject we must study well.

Strict self-cultivation is also a question of fostering and carrying out socialist core values.

Take self-cultivation as the first step and begin with it. We should use socialist core values, the highest common denominator, to bind the common understanding of society together and lead social conduct.

TWO

## WHY CULTIVATE MORAL CHARACTER?

> To become a good official, one needs to stringently comply with the Party Constitution and the requirements for Party members, which entails being 'strict with oneself and lenient with others'. Party members must always behave in a proper manner, scrutinise themselves, keep alert and encourage themselves (to avoid dazzling worldly temptations)."

> — XI JINPING

THIS EXCERPT IS from General Secretary Xi Jinping's speech at a National Organisation Work Conference, 28 June 2013.

### According to **Professor Wang Liqun:**

The maxim "Be strict with oneself and lenient with others" is from the *Book of Documents* (*Shang Shu*). That is currently viewed as meaning to be unsparing of oneself but broad-minded toward others. For a person who is cultivating their moral character, being either strict or lenient is a very difficult thing to achieve.

I have a historical story to prove the point. The story is from the *Biography of Lü Mengzheng* in the *History of the Song*.

Lü Mengzheng was a high-ranking and well-known official in the Song dynasty. His position was deputy prime minister. On his first day at work, he heard an official shouting loudly: "Is this guy the deputy prime minister?" Lü Mengzheng heard it clearly, but he pretended he had heard nothing. He continued walking as if nothing had happened. The others walking with him were very angry, complaining how the guy could speak in such a manner to the deputy prime minister. They wanted Lü Mengzheng to ask the official for his name. But Lü Mengzheng replied that he would never do it.

Because if he did, he would never forget this name. So don't ask and the matter comes to an end. Therefore he did not ask who the man was and the matter was over.

But the incident spread far and wide and many people marvelled at his broad-mindedness, therefore this minor incident was written down in the *Biography of Lü Mengzheng*.

Lü Mengzheng was also very strict with himself. After he became deputy prime minister, he held substantial powers. At the time one official was trying to ingratiate himself with Lü Mengzheng. He brought Lü Mengzheng a brass mirror, saying it was a treasure which could see things three hundred kilometres away and he was happy to give it to Lü. Lü Mengzheng told the official that his face was rather wide, but it was at most as wide as a plate. So why did he need a mirror that could see three hundred kilometres away? He refused to accept the official's gift.

The two incidents, one demonstrating broad-mindedness to others, and one being strict with himself, were just trivial things in Lü Mengzheng's life, but they were recorded in his biography. We can see that forgiving others but being unsparing of oneself is a very lofty realm of moral cultivation.

### According to **Professor Guo Jianning:**

Will being broad-minded lead to not being guided by principle? Or seeking good relations with all and sundry at the expense of principle? I think they are two distinct issues. Being strict with oneself and lenient with others does not mean that we don't want to adhere to principles, or even that we don't draw the line anywhere. We must be guided by principle, by Party spirit and draw the line somewhere. In practice we should unite the two aspects, being both strict with ourselves and lenient with others yet also guided by principle and Party spirit. Only by doing so can we do our work better.

# THREE
## HOW TO CULTIVATE MORAL CHARACTER?

" Young people should bear in mind that '*to follow what is right is like climbing a mountain, while following what is evil is like falling off a mountain*' and one should always be optimistic, a person of integrity and have a healthy lifestyle."

— XI JINPING

THIS EXCERPT IS from General Secretary Xi Jinping's speech at a seminar with teachers and students of Peking University, 4 May 2013.

### According to **Professor Wang Liqun:**

The saying "*to follow what is right is like climbing a mountain, while to follow what is evil is like falling off a mountain*" comes from *The Discourses of the States* (*Guo Yu*). It is well known in history, and also idiomatic, and is therefore a classic. What it stresses is that it is difficult to be good, but easy to do evil; it is difficult to improve, but easy to regress.

Let me use a historical story to explain it. In the *Book of Jin* there was a record of a man called Zhou Chu. One day, Zhou Chu asked his fellow villagers why they looked miserable after the village had bumper harvests for years running. His fellow villagers told him that although they had had bumper harvests for years running, they had had three pests to worry about. There was a tiger in the mountain, a dragon in the river and you, Zhou Chu, in the human world. If these three pests cannot be eliminated, there will be no peace in the world. After hearing these words, Zhou Chu said all right, he would go and eliminate these three pests. He went to the mountain and killed the tiger. Then he jumped into the river and fought with the dragon.

Drifting along the stream he swam dozens of kilometres. He fought with the dragon for three days and three nights until he was out of sight of the spectators. The locals all thought that Zhou Chu had died, so they beat drums, banged gongs and set off firecrackers to celebrate. But three days later Zhou Chu returned to the village. Seeing that the villagers were beating drums and gongs, he asked them why they were so happy. The villagers told him that they had heard he had died, so they were so happy that they set off fireworks to celebrate. Only then did Zhou Chu realise that he was actually one of the three pests. He thought that he had killed the tiger and the dragon, so he had to turn over a new leaf. He then went to Luoyang, the Western Jin's capital city, to see two of the most famous literary celebrities, Lu Ji and Lu Yun, who were Zhou Chu's fellow villagers in Dongwu. Lu Ji was not in, so Zhou Chu met Lu Yun. Zhou Chu said to Lu Yun: "I'm a grown-up. Can I turn myself into a better man?"

Lu Yun said: "Haven't you heard the old saying: 'If I hear the way in the morning, in the evening I can die content'? It means that if you hear a famous maxim in the morning, in the evening you can correct your wrongdoing; doesn't that mean you have turned over a new leaf?" Ever since then Zhou Chu mended his ways, and in the end he turned himself into a loyal and brave warrior.

The story of Zhou Chu illustrates one fact. To follow what is right is quite difficult, like climbing a mountain. To follow what is evil is rather easy, like falling off a mountain. But if we sincerely correct our shortcomings and errors, we can still achieve our life goals.

The ancient theory of self-cultivation was mainly about retraining oneself and cultivating one's integrity. What we are encouraging today is more suited to our ideals, convictions, moral sentiments and the lofty morals and noble character of Communists. The integration of all these shows that they meet the definition and requirements of the new era. We must combine cultivating moral character with an all-out effort to enforce strict Party discipline, which must always be practiced. Then there is no limit to our individual moral cultivation.

We must set a high standard and make strict demands on ourselves, so that we can build our integrity and become noble-minded to be of benefit to the people.

**part seven**

# Knowledge Originates from Practice

绝知此事要躬行

INTERPRETATION
IN PART 7 PROVIDED BY

-

**Professor Mao Peiqi**
*Renmin University of China*

*&*

**Professor Ai Silin**
*Tsinghua University*

# ONE
# VALUING ACTION

" As the saying goes: '*Success belongs to the realm of aspiration, and good business stems from hard work.*' Our country is still, and will be for a long time, in the early stages of socialism. To realise the Chinese Dream of rejuvenating the Chinese nation and creating a better life for all the Chinese people, there is tough work ahead and a long way to go. It requires every one of us to continue to put in hard work and great effort."

— XI JINPING

THIS EXCERPT IS from a speech delivered by General Secretary Xi Jinping at the First Plenary Session of the 12th National Congress, 17 March 2013.

### According to **Professor Mao Peiqi:**

The allusion to "*Success belongs to the realm of aspiration, and good business stems from hard work*" comes from the *Book of Documents (Shang Shu), which* is an important Confucian classic recording the history of ancient China. Under what circumstances was this maxim spoken? We know that there were the Xia, Shang and Zhou dynasties in ancient China. The Zhou dynasty replaced the Shang dynasty, destroying the Huaiyi people and returning to the capital Fengyi. King Cheng of Zhou warned his ministers and officials at all levels: "All you men of virtue, my occupiers of office, pay serious attention to your charges." What does this mean? It means that all officials must be careful with their jobs and matters they manage. Again King Cheng of Zhou said: "I warn you, my high ministers and officials, that exalted merit depends on aiming high, and a patrimony is enlarged only by diligence." What he wanted to tell his officials was that if they wanted to make great contributions, they had to have lofty aspirations; if they wanted to achieve something great, they had to focus their efforts and be diligent.

Therefore an aspiration cannot be just mentioned casually. It needs arduous efforts and diligent work to carry out a task persistently and solidly. Without effort and persistence, success cannot be achieved.

## According to **Professor Ai Silin:**

Then where does knowledge come from? From practice. Mao Zedong said: *"Genuine knowledge comes from practice"*. General Secretary Xi Jinping attaches great importance to practice. He stresses that practice is the source of theory, so he encourages investigation and research. He has said: *"Investigation and research are the basis of planning and the way to success. Without investigation and research, one has no right to speak, let alone decide."*

For example, it was during his investigation and research on the project for poverty alleviation that General Secretary Xi proposed that the government should take targeted measures. Since the 18th CPC National Congress, from east to west, from north to south, from the loess to the snow-covered plateaus, General Secretary Xi has travelled all over the country's impoverished areas, learning in detail about poverty-stricken families' situation regarding food, clothing, housing and travel, and during the course of this investigation and research he put forward the idea of taking targeted measures to alleviate poverty.

Second, whether knowledge is right or wrong is determined by practice or action. What is the criterion to decide whether a theory, an ideology or an understanding is right or wrong? Karl Marx gave a clear and definite reply in his article *Theses on Feuerbach,* that whether a theory is true or not can only be tested by social practice.

Since the 18th CPC National Congress, General Secretary Xi has clearly pointed out that all our work must withstand the examination of practice, the people and history. An official's ability and level of governance must be reflected in practice and tested in practice.

Third, skills and ability can only be increased in "action" and practice. As early as when Xi Jinping served as secretary of the Zhejiang Provincial Party Committee, he made a profound exposition. With regard to the training of reserve cadres, he said that we could not train them in hothouses but by sending them to places where conditions are harsh and the environment is complicated to temper them, to let them grow and to differentiate them. When in Liangjiahe Village, the young Xi Jinping did all kinds of work, such as carrying manure, tilling the land and building dams. In the eyes of the local farmers, Xi Jinping was a good lad who could endure hardship and work hard. Despite suffering a lot, Xi Jinping recalled later: "My experience in Liangjiahe benefitted me a great deal."

# TWO
## ACT QUICKLY

> A Chinese saying goes: '*A mountain is formed by the accumulation of earth and an ocean is formed by the accumulation of water.*' Happiness and a bright future will not appear automatically. Success only favours those with courage and perseverance. Let us dedicate ourselves to openness and win-win outcomes, bravely change and break new ground, and keep striving for a community with a shared future for humanity and a better tomorrow for Asia and the world."

— XI JINPING

THIS EXCERPT IS from General Secretary Xi Jinping's speech at the Opening of the Bo'ao Forum for Asia Annual Conference 2018, 10 April 2018.

### According to **Professor Mao Peiqi:**

The saying "*A mountain is formed by the accumulation of earth and an ocean is formed by the accumulation of water*" comes from the chapter of *The Achievements of the Confucians* in *Xunzi*. Literally it means that no matter how high a mountain, it is formed by the accumulation of handfuls of earth; no matter how deep an ocean, it is formed by the accumulation of drops of water. First, it shows that no matter whether a man is great or ordinary, he can only attain his lofty goal by making unremitting efforts.

Second, it tells us that when we do things, we must start well and end well. If the accumulation of earth or water stops halfway, can the mountain or ocean be formed? The answer is: "No."

There is another saying which we are all familiar with. In the *Strategies of the Warring States,* it says: "As the poem says: '*To cover*

74

*ninety per cent of one's destined distance brings the traveler no farther than the midway point.'* It tells us that the last part of a journey is the most difficult one." Later, this saying became an idiom. For a journey of a hundred and sixty kilometres, after you try for a hundred and forty-four kilometres, you have only done half the journey. Because the last sixteen kilometres are very difficult for you, as you are tired, and you have held on for too long and put in too much work. Although the destination is right in front of you, you begin to slacken your pace and in the end you waste all your efforts.

We all know that in *Xunzi* there was a saying: "*A journey of one thousand six hundred kilometres requires every step of the journey; an ocean or a river requires the convergence of every brook and stream. ... Carve but give up halfway, and even a decayed piece of wood will not break; work with perseverance, and metal and stone alike can be engraved.*" This is a wonderful saying, meaning that no matter how difficult a thing is, as long as you make unremitting efforts and are on the right path, you will realise your goal in the end. A river and an ocean need the accumulation of drops of water to form, and a mountain needs the accumulation of handfuls of earth to form, so a great undertaking needs to be started from every little bit.

<u>According to **Professor Ai Silin:**</u>

Yes indeed. But action does not mean to act rashly, and practice does not mean to practice blindly. So how can we do a good job?

First, we must persevere in doing our work. As the saying goes: "*One meal won't make a man fat*", nothing can be accomplished with a single effort. A successful practice is one that holds out to the last. So General Secretary Xi has stressed that apart from having a race-against-time enthusiasm, we must also have the tenacity to persevere. He used how Youyu County in Shanxi Province managed to control sand to illustrate this point.

Youyu County in Shanxi Province is situated in the Maowusu (Mu Us) desert. It is a natural wind tunnel and barren land. After New China was founded, the first Secretary of the county Party committee led the people to plant trees to control the sand. All his successors carried on with this project and this blueprint eventually turned the barren land into an oasis.

General Secretary Xi used this story to tell officials that they must have such a thought process that success is not necessarily achieved in one individual's term. As long as it is a scientific, reasonable programme, which conforms with reality and the will of the people, one after another they should carry on with it like running a relay race.

Second, we must rely on the masses. I am sure everybody has heard this proverb, "*One person can walk very fast, but a group of people can walk much farther.*"

Practice is not an individual but a mass activity, a social practice. No single individual can achieve anything significant. So General Secretary Xi stressed that our cadres and officials must improve their governance capacity. Where does the solution come from? From the masses. In 1984 when Xi Jinping served as secretary of the Party committee in Zhengding County, he wrote a letter to the county Party committee, People's Congress, government and Chinese People's Political Consultative Conference (CPPCC). He pointed out that they had to change their *Yamen* working style, go down to the grassroots, among the common people, to conduct investigation and research, take the masses as their teachers, and seek the source of running water from the people. He demanded that every year local officials devote one-third of their time to go down to the grassroots units to investigate and research. He himself had been to all the villages in the county. Because he had found the right issues to tackle and the measures were taken carefully, the local economy and society developed fairly quickly.

Third, work diligently. Hard work is the symbol of our Chinese nation, as the old saying goes, "*Greatness is achieved through diligence and retarded by laziness.*"

In 2018 when International Workers' Day was approaching, General Secretary Xi wrote back to the students of the class for model workers of the China University of Labour Relations. He said that labour is the greatest, most glorious, lofty and beautiful undertaking.

# THREE
## ACT DILIGENTLY

" Achieving the great renewal of the Chinese nation is a glorious and arduous undertaking that requires relentless joint efforts of generation after generation of the Chinese people. Therefore *'empty talk harms the country, while solid work makes it flourish'*. Our generation of Communists must carry forward the cause, inherit the past and usher in the future, and build our Party well to unite people of all nationalities in the entire country. We must build our country and develop our nation well and continue to boldly advance toward the historical goal of the great rejuvenation of the Chinese nation."

— XI JINPING

THIS EXCERPT IS from General Secretary Xi Jinping's speech at an exhibition on *The Road to Rejuvenation*, 29 November 2012.

### According to **Professor Mao Peiqi:**

The saying *"empty talk harms the country, while solid work makes it flourish"* comes from the *Records of Knowledge Gained Daily* by Gu Yanwu, a well-known thinker in the late Ming and early Qing period. The original text is as follows: "*Idle talk in the past was about Laozi and Zhuangzi whereas idle talk today is about Confucius and Mencius..... Relying on empty talk about how to discover and thoroughly understand one's true features to replace the practical learning of self-cultivation for better management of the common people, officials have no inclination to concern themselves with state affairs, therefore they have neglected government affairs. The army has no desire to fight battles, so all the areas outside the capital have turned to chaos. The Divine Land was invaded by tribesmen and the imperial court was overthrown. The country is in ruins!*"

*"The idle talk in the past was about Laozi and Zhuangzi"* indicated the regular practice of idle talk during the period of the Wei, Jin and the South and North dynasties (220-589AD). In those days the scholar officials talked about Laozi, Zhuangzi, as well as the New Daoism. This talk was totally unrealistic, having absolutely nothing to do with the national economy and people's livelihood.

*"The idle talk today is about Confucius and Mencius"*, this system of learning later developed into the Neo-Confucianism of the Song and Ming dynasties. After the Song dynasty, a group of Neo-Confucianist scholars specifically talked about the study of nature and the destiny of life, going to people's inner hearts to search for the truth, to search for the answer as to how to run a country. They abandoned real learning but transformed themselves into another kind of metaphysical thinkers. What happened after that? Ministers and officials neglected their duty of managing state affairs and did no practical work except to engage in idle talk about Confucius and Mencius, while office workers stopped doing any specific work. Therefore government affairs were neglected and the end result was the elimination of the state.

This saying was from the mouth of Gu Yanwu who lived in the time of the late Ming and early Qing dynasties. He witnessed the tragic demise of the Ming dynasty, which led him to reflect on the reasons for the Ming court's destruction. His conclusion was that one of the important reasons for the destruction of the Ming dynasty was that everyone in the country advocated idle talk. Therefore this example of idle talk endangering the country is a perennial lesson. Only practical work can make a country thrive, while empty talk leads the country astray.

### According to **Professor Ai Silin:**

Yes indeed. Without action, everything is empty talk, all claiming to lead to Utopia. Regarding the need to act diligently, I want to use three of General Secretary Xi Jinping's sentences to illustrate the point.

First, *"Socialism is built by hard work"*. Socialism is an unprecedented cause in human history. We can neither find it in a book, nor deduce it from theoretical logic, but rely on hard work to achieve it. There was a song in the 1950's film *The Young People in Our Village*. The lyrics were: *"Cherries are delicious, the tree is hard to grow. With no hard work, cherry blossoms will not come into bloom. Happiness does not come from the sky. Socialism cannot be built by waiting...."* General Secretary Xi has quoted these lyrics many times in his speeches. He wanted to tell the vast numbers of cadres, officials and the whole nation that socialism is built by hard work, not by waiting.

Second, *"The New Era is also built by hard work"*. In the report of the 19th CPC National Congress in October 2017, General Secretary Xi pointed out that after a long-term effort, socialism with Chinese characteristics has entered a new era. It is time for the Chinese people to strive for the realisation of the rejuvenation of the Chinese nation and to build China into a great modern socialist country which is prosperous, strong, democratic, culturally advanced, harmonious and beautiful. He said that we are closer than at any time in history to attaining the goal of the great rejuvenation of the Chinese nation, and we have greater confidence in, and capability for, achieving this goal than ever before.

However, we still face many challenges and difficulties that we must overcome. General Secretary Xi stressed that the rejuvenation of the Chinese nation can never be achieved easily. The closer we get to our goal, the less we should slacken our pace. We must work harder, roll up our sleeves and step up our efforts. The New Era needs men and women of action. General Secretary Xi himself is the greatest doer in this New Era. He advocates action above everything and getting things done immediately! There is a story about his 'immediate can-do mentality'. In 1991 Xi Jinping served as the Secretary of the Fuzhou Municipal Communist Party Committee. In view of the low efficiency of the Fuzhou Party Committee and the Municipal Government, he told the officials that matters regarding the Mawei Economic Zone had to be done immediately. Soon afterwards, the four words *"get it done immediately"* were hung in the courtyard of the Fuzhou

Municipal Party Committee to remind the vast number of cadres and officials that they had to dare to act, act quickly and raise work efficiency.

Third, "Youth is for struggle."

Indeed, everyone is young once in their life. Every generation of young people is offered the opportunities and missions of the era. What is the opportunity and mission for this generation of Chinese youth? General Secretary Xi said that the greatest opportunity, mission and test for them is to strive for the realisation of the Chinese Dream of the great rejuvenation of the Chinese nation.

This generation of young people is travelling in the New Era. Let us have a think, in 2020 when we build our country into a moderately prosperous society in all respects, those who are in their twenties today will be younger than thirty years old, and no older than forty when our country basically realises modernisation in 2030, and only fifty years old in 2050 when we comprehensively build our country into a modern and powerful socialist country which is prosperous, strong, democratic, culturally advanced, civilised, harmonious and beautiful. So it can be said that today's young people will participate in the whole process of the realisation of the Two Centenary Goals, therefore the young people must firmly bear in mind that working hard is their choice. Once they choose to work hard, they choose hardship, as well as harvests in the future.

In view of the development of history, some great thinkers, scientists and statesmen had their most important achievements in their youth. When the *Communist Manifesto* was published, Karl Marx was only thirty years old and Friedrich Engels was twenty-eight. When Issac Newton and Gottfried Wilhelm Leibniz discovered calculus, they were twenty-two and twenty-eight years old respectively. General Secretary Xi used these examples to tell young people that they must be resolute in making great efforts and show initiative, fighting spirit and dedication in the New Era, but not be wanderers or bystanders.

# part eight

# Ample Knowledge Instills Elegant Behaviour

腹有诗书气自华

ONE
## WHY LEARN?

" Learning is a prerequisite for growth and progress, while practice is the way to improve competence. The qualities and competence of young people have a direct impact on the course of realising the Chinese Dream. There is an old saying: '*Learning is the bow, while competence is the arrow*'. This means that the foundation of learning is like a bow, while competence is like an arrow; only with abundant knowledge can one give full play to one's competence. Young people are in the prime time of learning, so you should regard learning as a top priority, a responsibility, a moral support and a lifestyle. You should establish a belief that dreams start from learning and career success depends on competence. You should make assiduous learning a driving force and competence development a resource for your youthful endeavours."

— XI JINPING

THIS EXCERPT IS from General Secretary Xi Jinping's speech at the Symposium for Outstanding Youth Delegates from All Walks of Life, 4 May 2013.

### According to **Professor Meng Man:**

The adage "*Learning is the bow, while competence is the arrow*" comes from the *Sequel to Discourses on Poetry: Emphasise Learning* by writer Yuan Mei (1716-1797) of the Qing dynasty. The *Sequel to Discourses on Poetry* was a book about how to write poetry and the chapter *Emphasise Learning* was about the relationship between competence, learning, knowledge and insight. The more complete expression of this adage is "*Learning is the bow, competence is the arrow. Only when guided by knowledge and insight can the arrow hit the target.*" It means that learning is like the bow to exert force and competence is like an arrow to penetrate the shield. When you have the bow and the arrow, can you certainly hit the target? Not necessarily. There must be direction. The direction is knowledge and insight. Once you have knowledge and insight to guide you, after the bow exerts force and the arrow goes to penetrate, you can hit the target. In other words, we must take experience as the guide, knowledge as the foundation and talent as a spur.

General Secretary Xi Jinping alluded to the first half of Yuan Mei's maxim, which was about the relationship between competence and learning. In history it was a very important relationship and many scholars discussed it. Not only Yuan Mei, but historian Liu Zhiji in the Tang dynasty also talked about it.

Liu Zhiji said that having learning but no competence is like someone having one hundred *mu* (667 hectares) of good land but not knowing how to farm it and with no idea how to manage it. In the end you harvest nothing, and are unable to become rich. A talented person without learning is like a skilled carpenter who has neither wood nor axe, so he cannot build a house. That is to say talent and learning complement each other, neither can be omitted.

Young people find it easy to think that talent is more important than learning. Besides, they may be extremely frivolous, impatient and dislike the steady accumulation of knowledge and experience. But we must understand that we cannot achieve great deeds with talent alone. Let me use an example to illustrate this point. We have all studied Wang Anshi's famous essay *The Pity of Zhongyong*. Zhongyong could compose poems when he was five years old, showing he was a very intelligent child, or a little genius. Having blind faith in genius, his father was unwilling to send him to school to study, so in the end Zhongyong became a genius without a solid foundation in learning. His talent gradually withered. When he grew up, he was only able to be "just like ordinary people".

Let me give you an opposite example, the Tang poet Li Bai. Li Bai's nickname is 'Banished Transcendent', which means genius. Li Bai's talent was beyond question, but he also had a solid education. What books had he read? In his own words, "(I read) the elementary reader when I was five, and the Hundred Authors when I was ten". Only based on this solid foundation of learning, plus the supplement of his extraordinary talent could he achieve what poet Du Fu's description of him said: "When seeing him put pen to paper, the wind and rain sigh with feelings; when reading the poetry he composed, the ghosts and gods were moved to tears." And this is a perfect integration of talent and learning.

Let me go back to Yuan Mei's metaphor. Yuan Mei said that competence was the arrow. An arrow is very sharp, so people easily pay attention to its strength. But we must remember that the distance an arrow can go depends not only on the sharpness of the arrow, but more on the strength of the bow. Only through a strong bow can an arrow shoot farther.

As the ancient saying goes: "*No one is born wise or learned.*" In an absolute sense there is no genius in the world. Because of this, we should study hard and study all our lives, just as General Secretary Xi said, we should take learning as a responsibility, a lifestyle and a moral support, so solid learning can safeguard our glorious life.

### According to **Professor Xu Chuan:**

With regard to why we must learn, General Secretary Xi has earnestly spoken about four thoughts to interpret the reason for, and the significance of, learning. He said that learning is the way to inherit civilisations, the prerequisite for growth and progress, the basis for consolidation of political parties and the essential ingredient for the country's prosperity. These four dimensions are rich in levels and comprehensive in perspectives. "The way to inherit civilisations, the basis for consolidation of political parties and the essential ingredient for the country's prosperity" interpret from the macro aspect, namely, from the perspective of human civilisation, political party and state, while "the prerequisite for growth and progress" is interpreted from the perspective of individuality.

General Secretary Xi once mentioned a theory in modern talent science called the "theory of the rechargeable battery". It means that for modern-day talent, the time for it to be charged only once in its lifetime is gone. So we must be a highly efficient rechargeable battery. Only by constantly charging, can we achieve a continuous release of energy.

There are many stories about Liangjiahe, and today I am going to tell one.

In early 1969, Liangjiahe Village received fifteen secondary school graduates from Beijing, who were sent to the village for re-education. Enthusiastically the villagers helped carry their luggage. A clever young villager specially picked up a brown case which looked smaller in size and gradually he left the others behind. When they took a break half way, he went to try the larger cases, finding they were lighter than the case he was carrying. He so regretted selecting that case that he even mumbled to the others that it was as if he was carrying some gold, silver or treasure. Now we all know what was in the case. It was not gold or silver or a priceless treasure. It was a full case of books and the owner was Xi Jinping who hadn't even turned sixteen.

Seven years of life as an educated youth (referring to secondary school graduates who were sent to the countryside for re-education during the Cultural Revolution) in Liangjiahe not only enhanced Xi Jinping's ability, but also enriched his learning. It laid a solid foundation for his success in the university entrance examination. Relying on diligent study and an indomitable spirit, he truly changed his fate by reading and learning.

In 1975 Xi Jinping went to Tsinghua University, where he spent four years studying organic synthesis in the chemical engineering department.

After graduating from university, he went to work. No matter whether he served in Zhengding in Hebei Province or Xiamen in Fujian Province or Ningde, or headed the administration in Fujian, Zhejiang and Shanghai, including later becoming the leader of the Party and the State, the habit of reading and studying always accompanied him, which truly became the "prerequisite for growth and progress".

After the 18th CPC National Congress, Xi Jinping took on the post of General Secretary of the Central Committee and Chairman of the Central Military Commission of the Communist Party of China, as well as President of the People's Republic of China, beginning the much busier governance of the country. But his habit of reading and study never changed.

So General Secretary Xi's personal growth experience is a constant inspiration to us. No matter whether it is the young or the old, an individual or a political party, the masses or officials, or the cultivation of one's moral integrity or governing or serving, study is the most important thing to do. To put it briefly, each of us must study hard and make progress every day. And one is never too old to learn.

TWO

**LEARN WHAT?**

❝ Civilisations become colourful thanks to exchanges, and rich because of mutual learning and reference.

As a Chinese saying goes: *'He who studies alone in the absence of peers ends up being poorly informed.'* We should be ready to learn and borrow from all civilisations humanity has created, be they ancient Chinese, Greek, Roman, Egyptian, Mesopotamian or Indian civilisations, or today's Asian, African, European, American or Oceanian civilisations, and actively absorb their beneficial elements. We should make the outstanding cultural genes of all human civilisations adapt to and coordinate with contemporary cultures and present-day contexts, and advance and enrich the fine cultural spirit that transcends time and space, reaches across national boundaries, and has eternal charm and contemporary values."

— XI JINPING

THIS EXCERPT IS from a speech delivered by General Secretary Xi Jinping at the opening ceremony of the International Conference in Commemoration of the 2,565th Anniversary of Confucius' Birth and the Fifth Congress of the International Confucian Association, 24 September 2014.

<u>According to **Professor Meng Man:**</u>

The adage "*He who studies alone in the absence of peers ends up being poorly informed*" comes from the chapter *On Learning* from the *Book of Rites.*

*On Learning* was an essay specifically talking about education. It involved the topic of how to study well and why people failed to study well. It gave six possibilities for failing to study well and one of them was "*He who studies alone in the absence of peers ends up being poorly informed.*"

What is "*learning alone*"? It means learning alone with no friends to exchange views with. What could be the consequences?

Firstly, it could be 'ignorance', having a superficial knowledge of things. Secondly, it could be 'being ill-informed', having narrow horizons.

A person with superficial knowledge and narrow horizons can easily become a frog in a well, a narrow-minded person blinded by presumptuous self-conceit, which makes it hard for them to make any progress. Then how to solve this problem? It is easy. Can't we make friends and draw extensively on all useful opinions?

So-called making friends extensively does not mean making friends indiscriminately, but following what Confucius said: "*There are three types of friendship which are advantageous. Friendship with the upright; friendship with the sincere; and friendship with men with great powers of observation.*" That is to say we should make friends with those who are honest, experienced and knowledgeable, so that we can widen our field of vision, broaden the breadth of our minds and make progress.

We have now entered the age of the internet. If we want to learn from others, we don't need to experience the extreme hardships that Tang Seng experienced on his journey west to seek the '*Three Collections of Buddhist Scriptures*'. If we want to learn, we can do it without any difficulty at all. For this reason, we must make the best of the opportunity favoured by the times. The internet is so advanced. Rather than playing online games, we'd better draw on all useful opinions and make friends with people and civilisations around the world. During the course of this, we can constantly learn and grow to maturity. Only by doing so will we not fail the test of the times but live up to the expectations of General Secretary Xi Jinping.

# THREE
## HOW TO LEARN?

> The correct way needs to be pursued in practice, while morality requires no empty talk. One should be more pragmatic. Knowledge and action should go hand in hand, and the core values should be turned into a spiritual pursuit as well as a drive to make people engage in conscious action. The *Book of Rites* said: 'Learn extensively, enquire earnestly, think profoundly, discriminate clearly and practice sincerely.' Some people believe that 'sages are mediocre people who work hard, while mediocre people are sages who refuse to work hard.' Young people have more opportunities, so they should make their steps steady, lay a solid foundation and make unremitting efforts. In study or running a business, the worst danger is to be impulsive, work intermittently and change one's mind frequently."

— XI JINPING

THIS EXCERPT IS from General Secretary Xi Jinping's speech at a symposium with Peking University staff and students, 4 May 2014.

### According to **Professor Meng Man:**

The adage *"Learn extensively, enquire earnestly, think profoundly, discriminate clearly and practice sincerely"* comes from the chapter *The Doctrine of the Mean* from the *Book of Rites*. Tradition has it that *The Doctrine of the Mean* was written by Zi Si, the grandson of Confucius. The book was about the Confucian cultivation of human nature.

This excerpt of General Secretary Xi Jinping's speech is about the pursuit of study. How to pursue study? It should be to learn extensively, enquire earnestly, think profoundly, discriminate clearly and practice sincerely. They are five steps, or levels, for pursuing study and they have a progressive relationship with each other.

"*Practice sincerely*" is the highest stage of learning and also the real solution for all learning. Only by working hard in practice, and with knowledge and action going hand in hand, can our knowledge bring the most value into play.

In fact, if we have a careful think, we will see that these five learning methods are not only wonderful ways of learning, but also of living. In this complicated and changeable world we need the wisdom of learning extensively, enquiring earnestly, thinking profoundly, discriminating clearly and practicing sincerely to discover the truth. After we discover the truth, we need passion to throw ourselves into life and practice of the concept. Only by doing so can we practice truth and transform society. This is General Secretary Xi Jinping's expectation of the youth and of the times.

### According to **Professor Xu Chuan:**

Regarding study methods, General Secretary Xi has given us some suggestions and guidance.

The highest realm of study is like the description in the verse of *Yuanxi* to the tune of *Qing Yu An* by Xin Qiji (1140-1207): "*But in the crowd again I look for her in vain. When all at once I turn my head, I find her there where the lantern light is dimly shed.*" How to achieve this realm? General Secretary Xi has given us specific answers. It can be summed up in eight words: "*Combine learning with practice; integrate knowledge with action.*" How to follow them? Let us walk into the life of Tu Youyou, the scientist and researcher from the China Academy of Traditional Chinese Medicine, who is an example of combining learning with practice.

In 1967, in order to aid Third World countries, and also to eliminate a malaria epidemic in the southern region of China, Chairman Mao and Premier Zhou instructed Chinese scientists to urgently set up a team under military project jurisdiction to develop a new antimalaria drug. In 1969, thirty-nine-year-old Tu Youyou took part in the project. At the end of 1971 she identified material extracted from artemisinin as being a hundred per cent effective against plasmodium.

In 1981 the World Health Organisation held a conference in China, in which it highly praised the contribution artemisinin had made to the world.

At the time a French journalist asked Tu Youyou what she thought of the fact that, in the beginning, research into artemisinin was initiated because of war, yet now it was mainly used to save lives.

Tu Youyou replied: "I am very happy about it. As a medical scientist I must work to serve the health of humanity." Her goal was very simple. Learning was for application and application was to better promote learning. This was knowledge and action going hand in hand. We must pursue study, be good at study, be able to study, learn how to study, focus on study and enjoy study. We must study and believe, study and think, and study and act.

# part nine

# Evil Bamboo Should be Chopped Down in their Thousands

1. Dare not be corrupt

2. Cannot be corrupt

3. Not inclined to corruption

恶竹应须斩万竿

INTERPRETATION
IN PART **9** PROVIDED BY

-

**Professor Zhao Dongmei**
*Peking University*

&

**Kang Hui**
*TV Presenter*

&

**Huang Yibin**
*Central Party History and
Literature Office Researcher*

# ONE
# DARE NOT BE CORRUPT

" As a poem relates: *'New pines hate that they cannot grow a thousand feet tall; evil bamboo should be chopped down in their thousands.'* If evil is not entirely eradicated, it rises again from the ashes and makes a comeback at any rustling of change, which not only has a negative effect on political ecology, but also seriously damages the will of the Party and the people. Therefore, our pledge of enforcing strict Party discipline was not made casually. We will live up to our word."

— XI JINPING

THIS EXCERPT IS from a speech by General Secretary Xi Jinping at the 6th Plenary Session of the 18th CPC Central Commission for Discipline Inspection.

## According to **Professor Zhao Dongmei:**

The lines *"New pines hate that they cannot grow a thousand feet tall, evil bamboo should be chopped down in their thousands"* are from the fourth poem of the Tang poet Du Fu's *Five Verses I Composed for Mr Yan, the Duke Zhengguo, When I Was on My Way Back to the Thatched Cottage in Chengdu*. Mr Yan, the Duke Zhengguo, was Yan Wu, the son of a noted official.

Du Fu and Yan Wu were intimate friends. Du Fu left Chengdu and went to live elsewhere. After hearing that Yan Wu would come to Chengdu to govern Sichuan, he returned to Chengdu and this poem was written on his return journey.

Du Fu was very much looking forward to life in Chengdu. He wrote these poems to express his confidence and determination in rebuilding his home and new life after returning to Chengdu. He had left his home, the thatched cottage, for three years. In his imagination it had become dilapidated. What was Du Fu most concerned about? Four young pine trees he had planted with his own hands. He was hoping they would have grown as tall as a thousand feet. Then he thought that in the damp Chengdu climate, bamboo grew abundantly. Besides, bamboo could grow wild and spread everywhere. Du Fu wondered whether the bamboo could have hindered the growth of the pine trees. If it had, no matter how many had grown out of the ground, he was going to chop them down. When he thought about this, strong feelings of love and hate ran through his mind, so he wrote down, *"New pines hate that they cannot grow a thousand feet tall, evil bamboo should be chopped down in their thousands."*

We now use these two lines to express our determination that evil must be completely eradicated. If we want small pine trees to grow well, we must eradicate the evil bamboo. In fact, this is like the ethos of officialdom. If corruption and slack work cannot be eliminated, honesty and high efficiency cannot be established. Let me tell a story that happened in ancient times. When the Northern Song dynasty reached the eightieth anniversary of its founding, abuse of power had been endemic in official circles for years. The majority of officials reached their position after years of waiting. They took the official salary they were entitled to and also took what they were not entitled to. Yet they did none of the work they were obliged to do, therefore the whole official circle was overstaffed. Some people of noble aspiration put forward a proposal to the imperial court, saying that there had to be reform to purify the official ranks and clear out unqualified officials, particularly in leading posts. This was the *Qingli Xinzheng* reform movement we have all learned about from history books.

The men who led this reform were the Deputy Prime Minister Fan Zhongyan and the Vice Minister of the Privy Council Fu Bi. They decided that the first group of officials to be cleared out would be the *Lu*-level officials. A '*Lu*' was roughly equivalent to today's province. In Kaifeng, Fan Zhongyan held a registry book and examined the names. When he saw the name of an unqualified official, he picked up a pen and struck the name off the register. Fu Bi stood by Fan Zhongyan's side watching. He suddenly mentioned that ticking off a name was very simple, only a gentle tick, but when you committed your pen to paper, the official's whole family would cry. Hearing the remarks, Fan Zhongyan raised his head and looked at Fu Bi. Then he said seriously that if one compared one family's crying to the cries of all the common people, which one is more serious? The determination of the reformers was indeed like "chopping down thousands of evil bamboo", but it was a pity that this reform ultimately failed to achieve success. Yes, *"New pines hate that they cannot grow a thousand feet tall, evil bamboo should be chopped down in their thousands."* But it is not easy to completely eradicate evil.

### According to **Kang Hui:**

Of course, it is not easy to completely eradicate evil. Successive dynasties found that it was hard to accomplish this task. But if we don't resolve the problem, there will be endless trouble in the future. Therefore, no matter how difficult, we must do it, and make unremitting efforts to do it. We must have such determination.

General Secretary Xi Jinping alluded to these two lines of Du Fu's poem. He was in fact expressing such determination. We can say that strong determination is the primary driving force to combat corruption. Then where does this determination come from?

### According to **Huang Yibin:**

Many people have probed this question. In fact this determination comes from the responsibility to the future and the destiny of the Party and our country, and from whole-hearted feelings for the Chinese people. Here I would like to tell you a story about comrade Xi Jinping, which happened thirty years ago in Ningde Prefecture, Fujian Province.

At the time Ningde was a backward region. But in this backwater there was a 'phenomenon' that was 'not at all backward'. The local leadership was bent on violating discipline and breaking the rules to build houses for themselves on public land. The cost of this house building easily exceeded several hundred thousand yuan. At the time, the average annual salary for a worker in the province was about one thousand four hundred yuan. Where did the money and building material come from? Corruption. The practice of officials appropriating plots of land to build houses for themselves became more and more prevalent. Ordinary people had all but lost confidence in whether this evil practice could be brought under control.

But in 1989 things took a turn for the better. Before the new year of 1989, local leaders at all levels received a notice to attend a meeting. Some officials felt vaguely uneasy that a meeting had been convened at such a time. The person who presided over the meeting was Comrade Xi Jinping, who had just assumed office as secretary of the Ningde Prefecture Party Committee.

In the eyes of local cadres, this new secretary of the prefectural Party committee was amiable and approachable. But at the meeting that day they saw Xi Jinping sitting there quietly with a dignified expression. When talking about appropriating land to build houses, they said that it was a longstanding problem involving many cadres. So the best way forward was for the new official to treat it as a *fait accompli* and to let sleeping dogs lie.

Besides, some cadres said that it would be too difficult to tackle the problem as those who had built the houses were their colleagues, not to mention that laws fail if too many people disrespect them. If one confiscated the houses and the land, they would definitely be offended. Amid this atmosphere of conniving, evading responsibility and lack of principle, the young Xi Jinping angrily pounded the table and got to his feet. He said it was correct that the cadres involved were not small in number, but compared to the vast numbers of cadres they were a minority. Compared to the two million masses of people, they were even more of a minority. He affirmed that the problem had to be solved. He proposed an immediate freeze on all cadres' private housebuilding and that a comprehensive check to straighten things out be carried out immediately. Later in the *People's Daily*, there was a special report on this storm to clear up illegal housebuilding in the Ningde region, entitled "*Get One Job Done, Win the Hearts of the People*".

When Xi Jinping worked in Zhejiang Province, he continued to emphasise the importance of combating corruption with great force. After serving as the leader of the Party and the country, faced with severe and complicated anti-corruption work, he upheld a high-level, shock-and-awe policy. With an attitude of zero tolerance, he led the campaign to fight back against corruption, and to resolutely curb its spread and growth. After years of effort, what has been achieved is the preliminary realisation of the target that officials dare not be corrupt and a new look for Party and government conduct.

Now let us talk about the topic 'Cannot be corrupt'.

In the construction of an honest administration and the work to combat corruption, there is a saying: "Symptomatic relief gains time for radical treatment." Moves to combat corruption with force and to deter corruption are temporary solutions to the problem. What is the permanent cure? The permanent cure is institutional construction. Let us see what General Secretary Xi has to say about it.

# TWO
## CANNOT BE CORRUPT

" As the saying goes: *'Those who are good at exterminating evil examine its roots, those who are good at curing disease eradicate its cause.'* Our Party's long-term tenure of power gives us a huge political advantage, but also confronts us with a rigorous challenge. We must rely on the Party's organisations at all levels and the people's strength to constantly strengthen and improve our Party's construction, management and supervision."

— XI JINPING

THIS EXCERPT IS from a speech by General Secretary Xi Jinping at the 24th Collective Study of the Political Bureau of the 18th CPC Central Committee, 26 June 2015.

### According to **Professor Zhao Dongmei:**

The allusion to "Those who are good at exterminating evil examine its roots, those who are good at curing a disease eradicate its cause" comes from the Tang poet Bai Juyi's essay *Ce Lin*. What does *'Ce Lin'* mean? Literally it means forest of countermeasures. So it is a compilation of countermeasures. In other words, *Ce Lin* constituted Bai Juyi's ideas and suggestions to the government on political, military and economic issues.

The meaning of this allusion is very simple. It says that those who can find the root of a disaster are the ones who are truly good at exterminating it. Only those capable of finding the cause of a disease and then eradicating the cause are good doctors. To solve the problems faced by the state, Bai Juyi's proposal to the emperor was that the court take measures to carry out radical, thoroughgoing reform, starting with finding the source of the problems.

## According to **Kang Hui:**

This allusion is full of Chinese-style philosophy and wisdom. We know that doctors of Traditional Chinese Medicine never treat the head when the head aches, treat the foot when the foot hurts, or treat the symptoms but not the disease, but practice observation, auscultation and olfaction, interrogation, pulse feeling and palpation, so as to find the cause of the sickness and eradicate the cause. Therefore they treat a disease by looking into both its root cause and symptoms. Fighting corruption and advocating honest and clean government means looking into both its root cause and symptoms, and the cure is institutional construction.

Regarding institutional construction, General Secretary Xi has said a golden phrase which we are very familiar with. It is: "*To confine power in a cage of regulation.*" But how can we truly *confine power in a cage of regulation*?

## According to **Huang Yibin:**

First, we must build an effective cage of regulation. Second, we must have strong executive ability. Only by organically integrating both can "*confining power in a cage of regulation*" and institutional anti-corruption be achieved. All along General Secretary Xi Jinping has attached great importance to the institutional fight against corruption as well as institutional construction.

As early as thirty-five years ago, soon after Xi Jinping served as secretary of the Zhengding County Party Committee, he organised and drew up regulations to improve cadres' work style. Aimed at problems existing in the work style of local officials, requirements were put forward and institutionalised, producing a profound and lasting impact.

Since the 18th CPC National Congress, under the strong leadership of the Central Committee with comrade Xi Jinping at its core, a series of systems for managing people, things and money have been introduced. Within the Party, the focus has been on introducing, drafting and issuing laws and regulations concentrating on further perfecting the system, as well as further tightening the cage of regulation. It has promoted construction of the Party's work style and clean government, taking the treatment of both root causes and symptoms to a new level.

# THREE
## NOT INCLINED TO CORRUPTION

> Neither longevity nor seniority as a Party member automatically lead to the cultivation of Party spirit, theoretical consciousness or moral standing of an official. On the contrary, improvement requires a lifelong endeavour. To become a good official, one needs to constantly remould one's subjective world, and strengthen one's Party spirit cultivation and moral refinement. Party members must strive to keep alert to 'resist being swayed by the lure of small profit or being dizzied by the temptation of the five colours' and be honest and hardworking, clean and upright."

— XI JINPING

THIS EXCERPT IS from General Secretary Xi Jinping's speech at the National Organisation Work Conference, 28 June 2013.

### According to **Professor Zhao Dongmei:**

The maxim '*not to be swayed by the lure of small profit and dizzied by the temptation of the five colours*' is made up of two parts. Confucius said: "*Don't be impatient, and don't look for small advantages. If one is impatient, things will not be done thoroughly. Looking for small advantages prevents great affairs from being accomplished.*" What Confucius meant was that a ruler must respect the law of development, and at the same time not look for small profits. A ruler who looks for small profits has no way of achieving a lofty goal.

Let us look at the second part of the maxim. What are the '*five colours*'? The allusion to '*five colours*' originated from Laozi's *Tao Te Ching*: "*The five colours blind the eye, the five notes deafen the ear, the five tastes deaden the mouth.*" If we overindulge in things that are good to see, to hear or to eat, they will harm our vision or hearing and make us put on weight. Therefore we must not be lured or misled by appearances. This is actually what the ancient people refer to as "*be careful about minute details*".

"*Be careful about minute details*" was a very important principle for ancient Chinese scholars to cultivate their moral character and conduct themselves in society. For instance, we all know Bao Zheng (999-1062). In history, he was indeed an honest, upright and good official, a filial son and a loyal court official, which was hard to come by. Many of us can still recite his poem in which he expressed his high ideals: "*The root of managing officials lies in correcting their thinking, and uprightness is the principle of cultivating character. A good tree will be used as a ridge pole, and pure steel will not be used merely in the manufacture of hooks.*" As an official, Bao Zheng was always honest and upright.

How did he foster his charming character? He truly mastered being careful about minute details. He was never keen on gaining petty advantages but was strict with himself on every trivial matter. Before Bao Zheng was successful in the imperial examination at the metropolitan level, he reviewed his lessons with a classmate called Li in a temple in their hometown Luzhou.

Nearby lived a wealthy man who saw Bao Zheng and Li passing his house every day. He knew that the two were very good at their studies and that they definitely had a bright future, so he wanted to make friends with them. He often invited them to his house, but the two students declined his invitation.

One day the wealthy man decided to take action. He prepared a feast. Then he dispatched his housekeeper to invite Bao Zheng and Li to his house for dinner. It would have been ungracious not to accept the invitation, so Li was about to wash and get changed. Bao Zheng stopped him, saying that he could not go. The reason was that he and Li were scholars, and sooner or later they would become officials.

The wealthy man was inviting them for a meal today. If they accepted and gained benefit from him, if in the future they were appointed officials in their hometown, and if the wealthy man did something bad and came to them for help, it would have been difficult for them to uphold principle and turn him down. Listening, Li thought Bao Zheng was right, so he did not go.

Afterwards, they really did become officials in their hometown Luzhou. We know that in ancient times there was a system whereby officials were banned from serving in their own hometown. The fact that fellow students Bao Zheng and Li were able to return to their hometown to be officials, probably meant that they had excelled themselves in their official posts and that the emperor had every confidence in them. When they governed Luzhou, both did a very good job and were never troubled by human relationships. One can imagine that if they had gone to the wealthy man's feast and accepted gifts from him, after the first meal, there would have been a second and more gains. After they had succeeded in their imperial examinations, achieved wealth and power, and returned home to become local officials, the wealthy man would have been their benefactor. If the wealthy man had made requests to Bao and Li, there would have been no way they could have acted impartially for fear of offending him, and therefore no way for them to be upright in their posts.

Zhu Xi, a famous scholar in the Southern Song dynasty, attached great importance to this story. Because Zhu Xi had also been a local official, he knew what the stakes were in such a matter. He used the story of Bao Zheng and Li to teach his disciples, urging them to restrain their desires, to know what cannot be done, to have lofty aspirations, and to consider the consequences of anything they wanted to do. Only by doing so could they achieve *"not being swayed by the lure of small profit and dizzied by the temptation of the five colours"*.

In fact, in life, no matter whether it is Party members, cadres, officials or ordinary people, temptation is not just something you face when you are in a high position. Every one of us may be lured by temptation. Therefore we need to be strict with ourselves about every trivial matter and not be swayed by the lure of small profit, so that every time something major happens, we can be self-possessed and observe the law.

**part ten**

# Talent Rules Everything Under Heaven

天下之治在人才

INTERPRETATION
IN PART 10 PROVIDED BY

-

**Professor Kang Zhen**
*Beijing Normal University*

*&*

**Professor Wang Jie**
*Central Party School*

# ONE
## WHAT IS TALENT?

    As the saying goes: *'Talent supplements virtue, and virtue directs talent.'* Talent training must be a process of the unity of educating people and cultivating talent, and educating people is the essence. Without virtue, people cannot establish themselves in the world, so the essence of educating people lies in establishing their integrity. This is the dialectics of talent training."

— XI JINPING

This excerpt is from General Secretary Xi Jinping's speech at a seminar with teachers and students of Peking University, 2 May 2018.

### According to **Professor Kang Zhen:**

The saying *"Talent supplements virtue, and virtue directs talent"* is from the *Zizhi Tongjian* (*Comprehensive Mirror to Aid in Governance*): *The Record of Zhou* by Sima Guang (1019-1086), the great historian of the Northern Song dynasty. It means that morality and integrity lead talent, while talent and ability supplement morality and integrity. Let me explain the relationship between the two.

Why did Sima Guang say this in his book? Because there was a story that did not end very well.

During the Spring and Autumn Period (770-476BC), there was a senior state official called Zhi Xuanzi, who was searching for a successor to carry on his family business. He chose Zhi Yao, because he thought Zhi Yao was outstanding. However, among the clan members, Zhi Guo strongly opposed the idea. His reason was that Zhi Yao was indeed exceptionally talented and he possessed five merits: 1) he was tall, strong and handsome; 2) he was talented and skilful; 3) he excelled in horsemanship and was a formidable archer;

4) he was a decisive decisionmaker; 5) he had a glib tongue. All these merits showed that Zhi Yao was an outstanding man. But Zhi Guo said that Zhi Yao was absolutely not the man. Because although Zhi Yao had five merits, he had a fatal weak point which, when exposed, negated all five merits. What was his weak point? Lack of kindheartedness. Zhi Yao's integrity was flawed. Zhi Guo warned Zhi Xuanzi that if he let Zhi Yao be his successor to run the Zhi clan enterprise, the outcome would be disastrous.

As expected, Zhi Yao was greedy and without any benevolence. After he managed the Zhi clan, the whole clan suffered extermination.

So when Sima Guang talked about this story in his book, he made the comment: "*Talent supplements virtue, and virtue directs talent.*" How could Zhi Yao have led his clan to extinction? Because his talent overtook his virtue. In other words, his virtue failed to direct his talent, resulting in his failure. Sima Guang warned the common people that they usually could not tell the difference between ability and moral character, and they would jumble the two together. In short, they could think that a person was very able and virtuous, or that another person was very competent. Sima Guang said talent and virtue were not the same thing. Having virtue is having virtue, and having talent is having talent. Talent supplements virtue, and virtue directs talent.

Following on from this, Sima Guang made an important comment. He said: "If a man has both talent and virtue, he is a sage; if he has neither of them, he is a fool; if he has virtue but no talent, he can be called a gentleman; if he has talent but no virtue, he is a villain." To Sima Guang talent was no doubt important, but virtue was even more important. A man must have both virtue and ability, while taking virtue as the priority.

Sima Guang was not only a great historian, but also a great statesman himself. During the Yuanyou period in the Song dynasty, Sima Guang was the prime minister to Emperor Zezong. He promoted a talented person Liu Anshi to work at the secretariat. After Liu Anshi took office, Sima Guang had a conversation with him, asking him if he knew why he had been promoted. Liu Anshi said no, and that he was an honest person with no intention of ever soliciting connections. Sima Guang then said that when he was demoted by the imperial court and stayed at home doing nothing, Liu Anshi often came to see him to discuss problems with him. But after he became prime minister, Liu Anshi did not even write him a letter, let alone go to see him. With such conduct, he knew that Liu Anshi was a virtuous and upright man. Besides, he was truly competent, so he promoted Liu Anshi. In the *Zizhi Tongjian*, regarding virtue, Sima Guang clearly stated his views. He taught us a lesson with this historical story, while he himself earnestly practiced what he preached, setting an example for later generations.

## According to **Professor Wang Jie:**

Chinese culture attached great importance to virtue and moral value was paramount throughout history. The ancient Chinese made many comparisons to the relationship between talent and virtue. Some vividly compared virtue to *"the origin of a stream, the root of a tree"*, some compared talent to *"waves of water, leaves of a tree"*, or compared virtue to being *"the master of one family"* and talent to being a *"servant of the household"*. All these descriptions were to demonstrate that virtue was more important than talent.

After studying the series of important speeches by General Secretary Xi Jinping about talent, I think the following five points are the most important.

### 1) Love the country and the people.

Qian Xuesen once studied in the United States of America, where he had an excellent salary and living conditions. But after New China was founded, he broke through one obstruction after another and returned to his homeland.

We speak of science having no national boundaries, but scientists have their own homeland. From Qian Xuesen we can see his sincere and strong feelings of dedicating himself to the service of his country.

## 2) Ideals and convictions.

When Zhou Enlai was young, facing the imperialist powers invading China, slaughtering the Chinese people and killing Chinese civilisation, he was determined to 'study for the rise of China'. To us today, if we want to be successful, we must establish lofty ideals and goals, otherwise we will achieve nothing and get nowhere.

## 3) Do solid work and be willing to work hard.

Empty talk harms the country, while hard work brings prosperity to the nation. Li Baoguo (1958-2016) was praised as the 'New Foolish Man' on Taihang mountain, while someone called him the 'peasant professor'. As a professor of Hebei Agriculture University, he was busy teaching and doing research work. However he dedicated his whole life to the ordinary people.

According to statistics, in thirty-five years he held eight hundred training sessions and trained over ninety thousand people. Many of them who originally knew nothing about agricultural technology became extremely technically proficient. Li Baoguo used his talent, learning and hard-working spirit to erect a monument in the hearts of the people.

## 4) Reform and innovation.

Chinese culture stresses that *"if you can renovate yourself in one day, do so from day to day, and let there be daily renovation"* and *"when a series of changes has run its course, another change ensues; when it has free rein, it will continue for a long time."* All these sayings emphasise the importance of reform and innovation.

General Secretary Xi Jinping said: *"Only reformers can move forward, be strong and win victory."* It is all about the importance of reform and innovation. Yuan Longping, the 'world's father of hybrid rice' can be called an example of today's reform and innovation. For several decades he has worked unceasingly hard to perfect his skills regarding rice seedlings. He successively bred rice varieties with high and stable yields, making an inestimable and indelible contribution to China's grain security. Reform and innovation let him constantly move forward.

## 5) Taking on responsibilities.

General Secretary Xi Jinping has pointed out that *"the more responsibility one takes on, the more one can accomplish; the more one has done one's duty, the more one can achieve"*.

In the 1980s comrade Xi Jinping came to work in Zhengding County in Hebei province. He took a practical and realistic approach to work. He not only followed orders from above but adapted to the real circumstances, thereby laying a good foundation for the economic development of the county. To him, as long as the work was beneficial to the development of the county, no matter how difficult, he had to get it done and get it done well. What this embodies is taking on responsibility.

TWO
## HOW TO FOSTER TALENT?

" All past dynasties attached great importance to the selection and employment of officials. Long ago the ancients summed up the historical phenomena: '*The prime minister must have had experience as a prefectural official, and a valiant general must have been an ordinary soldier.*' In history, many eminent and noble-minded people began their official lives at county level."

— XI JINPING

THIS EXCERPT IS from General Secretary Xi Jinping's speech at a seminar with students of the Study Class of the Secretary of the County Party Committee, Central Party School, 12 January 2015.

### According to **Professor Kang Zhen:**

THE ADAGE "*The prime minister must have had experience as a prefectural official, and a valiant general must have been an ordinary soldier*" comes from *Hanfeizi: Xian Xue*. It means that if you want to be prime minister, you must first have worked at the grassroots levels of officialdom. If you want to be a general, you must first have served at the levels of squad, platoon, company and assistant general.

The growth of talent as well as cadres, is like tall buildings that are built from the ground up. The foundation is very important. If it is not solid, the higher the buildings are built, the quicker they will cave in when they collapse. Those who wish to achieve something great must start from the grassroots level. This is a very important view of Xi Jinping on cultivating talent.

## According to **Professor Wang Jie:**

Gaining experience at the grassroots level calls to mind what our ancient sage Laozi said: "*A tree so large that one person cannot get their arms around it begins as an insignificant sapling, a nine-storey tower is built one load of clay at a time, and a journey of a thousand miles begins with a single step.*" This means that high buildings are built from the ground up. The ground is the foundation. If the foundation is not solid, the earth shakes and mountains move.

In respect of cultivating talent, I have three points to make.

First, to become a talented person one must read and learn.

In November 2012 General Secretary Xi Jinping told a story. He said, one day a young man was at home wielding his pen passionately, in fact he was doing some translation work. Seeing that he was tired, his mother brought in some *zongzi* (rice dumplings eaten at the Dragon Boat Festival) and brown sugar, telling him that when he ate the *zongzi*, he should dip them in the sugar. He replied OK. A while later his mother returned to see if he had eaten the *zongzi*. He turned his head around and his mother saw that he had a black mouth. It turned out that rather than dipping the *zongzi* into the sugar he had dipped them in the ink and eaten them. When his mother asked him why he had a black mouth, he suddenly realised what had happened.

China's earliest Chinese translation of the *Communist Manifesto* was done by this young man. He was Chen Wangdao. Hence the saying: "*Truth tastes very sweet.*" That is to say one cannot become a talented person without reading and learning.

Second, to become a talented person one must temper oneself.

Competence comes from practice, and talent comes from experience and toughening. The numerous grassroots units are perennially fertile soil for fostering talent. From ancient to modern times, for those who achieved great undertakings, nearly all of them had the experience of working at the grassroots level. General Secretary Xi Jinping also proved it by his own experience of several decades.

When an official has the experience of working at the grassroots level, and when he makes decisions or thinks about how to solve problems, he can act in a down-to-earth manner, because he understands the people's livelihood and the country's conditions.

Third, for talent to grow, one must create a good environment and atmosphere.

General Secretary Xi Jinping said: "*When the environment is good, people with talent will gather and careers will be prosperous; when the environment is not good, people with talent will depart and careers will decline.*" This shows how important being surrounded by talent is to the cultivation of talent.

# THREE
# HOW TO UTILISE TALENT?

> As the saying goes: '*To accomplish extraordinary feats, one must wait for extraordinary people.*' Competent people are the most crucial factor for scientific and technological innovation. Innovative undertakings call for innovative talent. Respecting them has long been a fine Chinese tradition."

— XI JINPING

THIS EXCERPT IS from General Secretary Xi Jinping's speech at the opening ceremony for the 17th Academic Congress of the Chinese Academy of Sciences and the 12th Academic Congress of the Chinese Academy of Engineering, 9 June 2014.

### According to **Professor Kang Zhen:**

The maxim "*To accomplish extraordinary feats, one must wait for extraordinary people*" comes from the *Book of Han: The Biography of Emperor Wu* by historian Ban Gu in the Han dynasty. What was the background for this adage? In the fifth year of Yuanfeng, which was in 106 BC, Emperor Wu issued a decree, calling all prefectures to recommend talent to the imperial court. What kind of talent did the emperor want them to recommend? To accomplish extraordinary feats, the court had to have, and to wait for and rely on, extraordinary talent.

In fact this maxim had a history. Twenty years prior to the fifth year of Yuanfeng, Sima Xiangru (179-118 BC), the famous literati and writer of Han *fu* (descriptive prose interspersed with verse) in the West Han dynasty, submitted a memorial to Emperor Wu to discuss the issue of defence in the southwest border region. He used the word 'extraordinary' five times to present his opinions which read:

*"Extraordinary people are the prerequisite for extraordinary feats, only after doing extraordinary deeds can a person make an extraordinary contribution, therefore an extraordinary person is different to an ordinary person."* Emperor Wu paid great attention to the five mentions of the word 'extraordinary' and twenty years later he summarised them as *"to accomplish extraordinary feats, one must wait for extraordinary people."*

## According to **Professor Wang Jie:**

I have three points to make on how to utilise talent.

First, we must adhere to the correct guidance of making use of people. General Secretary Xi said that the guidance of choosing a person for a job is the most important, basic and effective thing. When the prefectures and counties are managed well, the country is at peace. General Secretary Xi has attached great importance to the construction of the ranks of county Party secretaries. In 2015 the CPC Central Committee commended 102 county Party secretaries, and soon afterwards some of them took on a higher-level leading post. Liao Junbo (1968-2017) was one of them. He cared for the masses, and led the local Party members and cadres to work hard in real earnest. As an official, he was open-minded, upright and honest. As a family member, he urged his other family members not to seek privilege but to work harder and contribute more to society. Therefore he was a monument in the hearts of local Party members and officials. Many local people and Party members and cadres still miss him very much when he is mentioned.

I think under the correct guidance, more leading cadres like Liao Junbo will emerge in modern Chinese society.

Second, choosing a person for a job should avoid their weak points but make use of their strong points. There is sediment in every wine. General Secretary Xi pointed out that deciding who to appoint to what post must be determined by the need of the work. Selection should be made according to the job in question, a post should not simply be used as a means of rewarding a cadre. He also quoted a poem of the Qing poet Gu Sixie to underscore the point: "*A good horse can run along dangerous paths, but it cannot plough fields like an ox; a strong cart can carry heavy loads, but it cannot cross rivers like a boat.*" Because everyone has their own strengths and weaknesses, only by utilising their strengths can we bring out the best in people, or the consequences will be very serious.

Third, select talent of all kinds. Since ancient times, all those with foresight have advocated not sticking to one pattern when selecting talent. Today, when we select somebody for a job, we must not overemphasise whether they have formal schooling, status, qualifications or a record of service, but be broad-minded, and willing to appoint people on their merits and recruit people of intelligence and integrity from all corners of the land.

**part eleven**

# Bite the Green Mountains Tightly and Don't Let Go

1. Why the need for ideals and beliefs?

2. What kind of ideals and beliefs should be established?

3. How to uphold ideals and beliefs?

咬定青山不放松

INTERPRETATION
IN PART II PROVIDED BY

-

**Professor Meng Man**
*Minzu University of China*

*&*

**Professor Xu Chuan**
*Secretary of the CPC General Branch of the School of Marxism*
*Studies, Nanjing University of Aeronautics and Astronautics*

# ONE
## WHY THE NEED FOR IDEALS AND BELIEFS?

" Ideals and beliefs refer to people's aspirations. As one of the ancients said: *'Aspiration can reach any place however far it is, even over mountains and seas; and it can break through any defence however tough it is, even if it as strong as the best armour and shield.'* This shows how strong and invincible people can be if only they have lofty ideals. During China's revolution, development and reform, innumerable Party members laid down their lives for the cause of the Party and the people. What supported them was the moral strength gained from the utmost importance they attached to their revolutionary ideals."

— XI JINPING

THIS PARAGRAPH IS from General Secretary Xi Jinping's speech at the National Conference on Organisational Work, 28 June 2013.

### According to **Professor Meng Man:**

The maxim in this paragraph is from *Collected Maxims* compiled by Jin Ying, a Qing dynasty scholar. *Collected Maxims* is the equivalent to today's 'encyclopaedia of well-known sayings and adages'. Why did General Secretary Xi allude to this maxim? He was talking about being determined to do things when he quoted it.

We often talk about 'lofty aspirations'. Well, how high-minded can aspirations go? According to *Collected Maxims*, there is no place one does not go. An idiom from the original text of the *Book of Documents* reads: "*There is nothing too far out of reach that the virtuous cannot obtain.*" It means that moral integrity can move heaven and earth and no place is too far away to be touched by morality and virtuous conduct. In fact, not only moral integrity, but aspiration has such power too. Then how high-minded can aspiration go? *Collected Maxims* gave us two specific images, one being over the mountains and one being over the sea, 'the end of the sky' and 'the four corners of the sea' in our sayings. Wherever our aspiration goes, even reaching the mountains and the sea, as long as we are determined to move forward, neither the mountains nor the sea can prevent us from achieving our goal. And this is about the degree of distance.

The second part of the maxim is about intensity. *"It can break through any defence however tough it is, even if it is as strong as the best armour and shield."* The saying *"it can break through any defence however tough it is"* is also an idiom. We usually talk about 'being all conquering', which means that there is nothing solid that cannot be destroyed. What are the solid things? The author of *Collected Maxims* gave us two specific images: sharp weapons and top-quality armour. What is aspiration before sharp weaponry? It is armour. No matter how sharp a weapon is, it cannot break through the armour. What is aspiration before armour? It is a sharp weapon. No matter how strong the armour is, the sharp weapon can certainly break through it. That is to say no substantial force is strong enough to resist the force of aspiration.

Why does aspiration possess such great power? It is quite simple. A grand term for aspiration is ideal, while an unimposing term for it is a goal. Only by having an ideal or goal, can one have the aspiration and courage to go and do things ordinary people think are unimaginable.

For example, the *Book of Later Han: Biography of Geng Yan* tells a story about General Geng Yan. In the late years of the Western Han dynasty, when the whole country was in chaos, Geng Yan was a twenty-one-year-old young man. He went to Liu Xiu (founder of the Eastern Han dynasty) in Nanyang and joined his rebel forces. He urged Liu Xiu to recover the lost Hebei from where they could crush the imperial court forces, and thereby bring peace to the country. At the time, Liu Xiu had only a small force, while Geng Yan was a little-known young man, so everyone felt that his talk was completely exaggerated, and impossible to realise. However, as Geng Yan had such an aspiration, he produced death-defying courage.

For instance, when they attacked Shandong, Geng Yan was hit in the leg by an enemy arrow. Pulling out his sword, he cut the head of the arrow off and carried on fighting. Because of his courage and disregard for his own safety, he turned into a truly unbeatable general. His goals, whether to recover Hebei, to defeat the imperial court forces, or to help Liu Xiu bring peace to the country, were all realised. So looking at him, Liu Xiu sighed with emotion: "Where there's a will, there's a way." This is where the idiom we are familiar with comes from.

In fact, as well as the story of Geng Yan, we are also familiar with stories such as that of King Goujian of the Yue State who underwent self-imposed hardships so as to strengthen his determination to wipe out the national humiliation; Sima Qian firmly resolved to write the *Records of the Grand Historian*, and Zu Di vowed to annihilate the rebels. The reason they succeeded where others failed was because they had the aspiration to pluck up their courage and willpower.

When General Secretary Xi alluded to this quotation, he was talking about the establishment of lofty ideals. No matter whether in the years of the revolutionary wars or the reform, we all need to have ideals and beliefs. We all need to use ideals and beliefs to inspire our will to fight, so that we can reach anywhere, no matter how far, and break through any defence, no matter how tough.

## TWO
## WHAT KIND OF IDEALS AND
## BELIEFS SHOULD BE ESTABLISHED?

Traditional Chinese culture is both extensive and profound, and learning and acquiring the essence of its various ideas is beneficial to the formation of a correct world view, outlook on life and sense of values. Our forefathers stated that our aspirations should be as follows: in politics, '*being the first to worry about the affairs of the state and the last to enjoy oneself*'; as patriots, '*not daring to ignore the country's peril no matter how humble one's position may be*', and '*doing everything possible to save the country when it is in danger without regard to personal fortune or misfortune*'; on integrity, '*never being corrupted by fame and fortune, never departing from principle despite poverty and coming from humble origins, and never submitting to force or threats*'; on selfless dedication, '*dying with a loyal heart shining in the pages of history*' and '*giving one's all until the heart beats its last*'. All these sayings reflect the fine traditions and spirit of the Chinese nation. We should keep them alive and further develop them."

— XI JINPING

THIS EXCERPT IS from General Secretary Xi Jinping's speech at the Central Party School's ninetieth anniversary celebration as well as a ceremony marking the start of the spring semester, 1 March 2013.

### According to **Professor Meng Man:**

The allusion to "*not daring to ignore the country's peril no matter how humble one's position may be*" is a famous saying of Lu You (1125-1210), the prominent patriotic poet of the Southern Song dynasty. It is from his verse *My Written Aspirations After Recovery From Illness*. The poem itself was not particularly popular, but the line "*not daring to ignore the country's peril no matter how humble one's position may be*" is the crux of the verse. Everyone knows it and is touched by it.

We all know that Lu You was a patriot. He was born during a time of military confrontation between the Song court and the Jurchen people from the north of China. Throughout his life, Lu You wanted to recover the lost land. But the Southern Song regime had neither the guts nor the strength to carry out a northern expedition, so Lu You constantly submitted to the imperial court the request to be granted a military assignment. His efforts failed and he kept being dismissed from office. This poem was written on the occasion of one such dismissal from office.

If an ordinary person was dismissed from office and fell ill, would they feel sorrowful? Certainly they would, and so did Lu You. However, Lu You's sorrow was not for his own future and destiny, but for "the countrymen in the north expecting the emperor to personally lead his soldiers to recover the lost land", and because "*everything turns to dust in my dying eyes, hatred is the only reason a unified land is not seen.*" Lu You was still alive when he wrote this verse. He was indignant and in grief. He asked when the country could be reunified? So his grief was not ordinary grief, but a concern for the future and destiny of the country and the nation. He was care-laden. Was he an emperor? Of course not. Was he the prime minister? Not that either. He was just an official who had been dismissed from office, a man with no power or influence. But he persevered despite knowing it could not be done. This is what "*not daring to ignore the country's peril no matter how humble one's position may be*" means, and this represents great spiritual strength.

When it came to the time of the later Ming and early Qing dynasties, a great thinker called Gu Yanwu said: "*Protecting the whole country concerns the life-and-death struggle for the nation as well as the cultural inheritance, and therefore every ordinary man's duty and obligation."* This sentence was later refined by Liang Qichao as: *"Every man shares responsibility for the fate of his country."* So it is this quiet undertaking of responsibility that made the Chinese nation straighten its back. And this spirit deserves to be carried forward forever.

# THREE
## HOW TO UPHOLD IDEALS AND BELIEFS?

> Our whole Party must strengthen our confidence in the path, theory, system and culture of socialism with Chinese characteristics. We must neither retrace our steps to the rigidity and isolation of the past, nor take a wrong turn by changing our nature and abandoning our system. We must maintain our political orientation, do good solid work that makes our country thrive, and continue to uphold and develop socialism with Chinese characteristics.
>
> We must strive to achieve *'remain hard and strong after one thousand buffetings and ten thousand beatings, no matter whether the wind blows from east, west, south or north.'*

— XI JINPING

THIS EXCERPT IS from the 19th CPC National Congress Report delivered by Xi Jinping, 18 October 2017.

### According to **Professor Meng Man:**

The famous calligrapher, painter and poet Zheng Banqiao in the Qing dynasty composed the well-known poem *Bamboo and Rock*. It reads: "*Bite the green mountain tightly and don't let go; they take root amid rugged rocks. Remain hard and strong after one thousand buffetings and ten thousand beatings; no matter whether the wind blows from east, west, south or north.*" The verse was not written about real bamboo and rock but was inscribed on the painting "*Bamboo amid Rocks*", so it was a poem in a painting.

We know that Zheng Banqiao was a representative figure of the "Eight eccentrics in Yangzhou", so he was a weird man in his life. For instance, he said he would only paint orchids, bamboo and stone, and what he painted were not ordinary orchids, bamboo and stone, but *"the orchid that never withers in the four seasons, the evergreen bamboo that grows a hundred joints, the stone that never decays and the person that does not change for a thousand years."* As soon as we hear these lines, we know that his paintings are not European still-life drawings, but Chinese-style freehand brushwork. In other words, his bamboo poems and paintings were not just about bamboo plants, but more about the spirit behind them.

What spirit? The heart of it is its staunchness, and natural and unrestrained manner. Where does the staunchness lie in the verse? It lies in the word *'Bite'*. Does the bamboo have good earth to grow in? No, the ground is not good at all. The bamboo does not grow in fertile soil, but takes root in rugged, broken rocks on the mountain, and grows through cracks in the rocks. However, it bites the green mountain tightly, never letting go. It is determined to survive on the mountain rocks and stand erect. What a firm and staunch spirit this is!

The second characteristic of the verse is its natural and unrestrained manner, which lies in the character *'ren'* (任, literally meaning 'no matter what' or 'any'). We know that bamboo growing on mountain rocks receives no care from people. When the wind blasts and the rain hammers down, bamboo has to withstand the natural elements. It is precisely such buffeting and beating by wind and rain, that fosters and capitalises on bamboo's carefree and unrestrained disposition. That is *"no matter whether the wind blows from east, west, south or north"*. No matter from which direction the wind and rain comes, I will stand tall and upright. This is a natural and unrestrained manner! This is the manner of the Chinese people, being independent and resolute!

### According to **Professor Xu Chuan:**

After Meng Man's explanation, we should be clear why bamboo can remain staunch and stand upright after one thousand buffetings and ten thousand beatings in the wind and rain. The answer is in the first line: *"Bite the green mountains tightly and don't let go"*. In fact, the character of bamboo is like the moral quality of a human being. Only by taking root deeply in rocks on mountains can it maintain steadfastness and uprightness when facing the elements and hardships. This equally applies to humans. Only by strengthening our convictions and corroborating our beliefs, can we *"avoid regret despite dying nine times"*, or *"keep travelling east in spite of all setbacks"*.

Where does belief come from? From theory, as well as practice.

First, our belief comes from theory. The salvoes of the October Revolution brought China Marxism. The wandering Chinese discovered that we could rely on neither emperors, generals or ministers, nor warlords nor financial groups, but the people who were the most reliable force. Just as we all know, the people, and the people alone, are the motive force in the making of history. This theory germinated in Karl Marx's *The Holy Family* is perfectly integrated with the reality of China.

Second, our faith comes from practice. The Chinese Communists combined Marxist basic theory with the practice of the Chinese revolution and construction. We stood up, which proves that only socialism can save China. The Chinese Communists combined Marxist basic theory with the practice of the Chinese reform and opening up. We are prosperous, which proves that only socialism with Chinese characteristics can develop China. The Chinese Communists combined Marxist basic theory with the actual Chinese conditions in the new era. We have realised the great leap forward of becoming powerful from becoming prosperous, which proves that only by maintaining and developing socialism with Chinese characteristics can we realise the great rejuvenation of the Chinese nation.

We all believe that happiness is obtained by hard work. We all believe that we are the masters of our own destiny. Every Chinese has a dream of building China into a powerful country, and every Chinese must not forget that our happy life today has not come easily.

**part twelve**

# When the Great Way Prevails, all Under Heaven will be one Community

1. Make extensive friendships

2. 'One Belt, One Road'

3. Building a community with a shared future for humanity

天下為公行大道

INTERPRETATION
IN PART 12 PROVIDED BY

-

**Professor Kang Zhen**
*Beijing Normal University*

&

**Professor Wang Jie**
*Central Party School*

ONE
## MAKE EXTENSIVE FRIENDSHIPS

> Confucius, a Chinese philosopher, said over 2,000 years ago: *'It is such a delight to have friends coming from afar.'* It expressed the joyful feeling of the Chinese people at the arrival of friends. We have invited friends from home and abroad to gather together here so that we can thank you for your unremitting efforts in enhancing the friendship between China and other countries, review our extraordinary journey in pursuit of our common aspiration, and celebrate our longstanding friendship and cooperation."

— XI JINPING

THIS EXCERPT IS from a speech delivered by General Secretary Xi Jinping at the China International Friendship Conference and the Commemoration of the Sixtieth Anniversary of the Founding of the Chinese People's Association for Friendship with Foreign Countries, May 2014.

### According to **Professor Kang Zhen:**

The maxim *"It is such a delight to have friends coming from afar"* is from *The Analects of Confucius.* The original text reads: "(The Master said:) *'Is it not a pleasure, having learned something, to try it out at due intervals? Is it not a joy to have friends come from afar? Is it not gentlemanly not to take offence when others fail to appreciate your abilities?'"*

The word *'friends'* here means crowds. We know of a proverb *"Things of one kind come together, people of a kind fall into the same group".* Confucius's original meaning was that when people cherishing the same ideals and following the same path came to gather around him from all directions, wasn't it a joyful thing? In Confucius' time, people perceived that if they wanted to achieve something, particularly to accomplish some great deeds, they had to have people who shared common ideas to work with. Only by working with such people, could they feel happy, and be valued for their achievements.

It is said that Confucius had three thousand disciples from all places. They had different personalities and the difference in age was also great. The eldest one was the same generation as the youngest one's father. For the large numbers of different types of students, the teaching method adopted by Confucius was to provide education for all without discrimination. All men were brothers. Confucius gathered them around his lecture room, the Xing Tan Pavilion, forming a spectacular scene of education. At the time he trained a large amount of talent for society. Therefore we can say that *"it is such a delight to have friends coming from afar"* is a call for friends, a welcome to friends, but more Confucius's impressive way of calling for talent.

Not only did Confucius say that *"it is such a delight to have friends coming from afar"*, but he also offered his opinion on what kind of friends people should make. For example, he thought that people should make more friends who were helpful, but less friends who were harmful; make more friends who could treat you sincerely, help you with knowledge, morality and integrity, but not make friends with those who would do crooked things and harbour evil intentions. He also thought that people should treat friends sincerely and keep their word. His disciple Zi Xia said one should be faithful in contact with friends. In fact, in present-day life, the most used idioms and proverbs on making friends all come from Confucius and his disciples. Confucius also advocated that when making friends, attach importance to righteousness rather than profits, and assist humanity by friendship. He said: *"The superior man thinks always of virtue; the common man thinks of interests."* What does this mean? When making friends, a true superior man relies on justice, common ideals and beliefs, but a common man only takes into consideration interests or material gains.

This adage of Confucius shows us the values of the Chinese nation in treating friends, friendly countries, the world and different nationalities.

General Secretary Xi Jinping used this adage to lay out clearly for people around the world China's position and values when we make contact with them. We will open our door to them and make friends with them if they are willing to communicate and cooperate with China. Only with this course of action can we let the people of the world understand China, while we further our understanding of the world.

# TWO
## "ONE BELT, ONE ROAD"

> The ancient Chinese philosopher Mencius said: '*Ensuring the right conduct and upholding justice should be the way to follow across the land.*' We call on all parties to join the circle of friends for the 'Belt and Road Initiative'; instead of attempting to fill the 'vacuum', we are building a cooperative partnership network for a win-win outcome."

— XI JINPING

THIS EXCERPT IS from a speech delivered by General Secretary Xi Jinping at the Arab League Headquarters, 21 January 2016.

### According to **Professor Kang Zhen:**

The adage "*ensuring the right conduct and upholding justice should be the way to follow across the land*" is from *Mencius: Teng Wen Gong II*. The background to this maxim is that Jing Chun, a political strategist, was Mencuis' disciple. He discussed the issue of great men with Mencius. In Jing Chun's eyes, political strategists, such as Gongsun Yan and Zhang Yi, were great men. Because when they were angry, the world was in turmoil, while when they were quiet, the world was at peace. But Mencius did not think that they should be considered as great men. He pointed out: "*A true man lives within the most extensive home of 'benevolence', stands in the most upright position of 'propriety', and walks the broadest path of 'righteousness'. If he is able to achieve his ambitions, may he do so with the people. If he cannot, may he hold firm to his principles. Wealth or honour do not corrupt him, poverty or humble origins do not motivate his ambition, and armed coercion does not force him to submit. This is what constitutes a true man.*" This exposition of Mencius can be described as extraordinary, truly representing compliments to the great men in Chinese history who conducted themselves in a just and honest way.

Mencius' theory as well as the integrity of a great man has also become a very important principle of ours in establishing our image as a great power internationally. Just as General Secretary Xi Jinping has said that we do not act as agents, nor seek to fill some so-called 'vacuum'; we are willing to achieve a situation of mutual benefit and win-win with other countries and the people of the world; we are willing to build a community with a shared future for humanity so that on the foundation of mutual benefit, win-win and mutual trust, together we can build a beautiful global homeland. I think it is China's fine traditional culture that has given us confidence in our socialist culture, system, theory and path.

## According to **Professor Wang Jie:**

Let me talk about the 'Belt and Road Initiative'. Chinese culture has always sought the diplomatic aim of a diverse and harmonious world, taking into account the public interest, cooperation and shared victory, with each appreciating their own beauty and magnanimously appreciating the beauty of others, integrating one's own beauty with that of others and realising the ideal of Great Harmony. Only by achieving mutual benefit, cooperation and shared victory can we obtain the result of one plus one being greater than two. As Confucius said, "*A benevolent man, wishing to establish himself, sees that others are established, and wishing success for himself, sees that others are successful.*"

We had such a case regarding Zheng He, the greatest navigator in Chinese history. His voyages (1405-1433) to the Western Ocean (Indian Ocean) displayed the cultural spirit of peace and friendship, and living in mutual harmony. Now in Thailand there is a gold-plated statue of Zheng He, and relics of Zheng He's treasure ships are on display in the Maritime Experience Museum in Singapore. This is strong evidence of China's friendly contacts with foreign countries.

When calculating interest, we should not only calculate our own interest, but that of the whole world. Zheng He's voyages to the Western Ocean were the best example of this viewpoint.

General Secretary Xi pointed out that space is spacious enough and the planet is large enough to accommodate the development and prosperity of all the world's countries. In today's world, no one can pay attention only to their own interests without thinking of others. No country can develop without contact with other countries.

General Secretary Xi initiated the principles of extensive consultation, joint contribution and shared benefit for global governance, which is in line with the pulse of the times and points to a bright way for win-win cooperation to solve the challenges of globalisation.

# THREE
## BUILDING A COMMUNITY WITH
## A SHARED FUTURE FOR HUMANITY

> " Living things that are nourished do not injure one another; roads that run parallel do not interfere with one another. We need to stand at the perspective of world history and examine the development trends and the problems we face in the world today, continue to pursue a path of peaceful development, an independent peaceful foreign policy, and a mutually beneficial strategy of opening up. We need to continue to expand cooperation with all other countries, take an active part in the global governance system, and realise mutually beneficial cooperation and shared development in more fields and to a higher level, and we must not submit to others, less still plunder others. In this way, we can work with the people of all other countries to build a community with a shared future for humanity and create a more beautiful world."

> — XI JINPING

THIS EXCERPT IS from General Secretary Xi Jinping's speech at the Commemoration of the Two-Hundredth Anniversary of Marx's Birth, 4 May 2018.

### According to **Professor Kang Zhen:**

The adage *"living things that are nourished do not injure one another; roads that run parallel do not interfere with one another"* comes from the Confucian classic *The Doctrine of the Mean*. It means that all things on earth grow together. Although in the same environment, none interferes with the growth of others. We run parallel but do not interfere with one another.

There is a saying in *The Analects of Confucius*: "*In practicing the rule of rites, it is harmony that is prized.*" What are "*rites*"? In the Spring and Autumn Period, "*rites*" meant moral standard, or norms of conduct. The saying means that if everyone collectively observes a certain regulation, or a notion and maintains a certain order, people can create a win-win situation, can coexist and achieve joint development. This is the conclusion our ancestors came to after summarising methods of running the country and certain rules governing the development of human society.

General Secretary Xi Jinping has proposed that we build a community with a shared future and a harmonious world. During the course of this activity, if the criterion of "*peace is of paramount importance*" and the philosophy of "*living things that are nourished do not injure one another; roads that run parallel do not interfere with one another*" are applied to present-day international relations, it will lead to a truly creative and innovative development of fine traditional Chinese culture.

## According to **Professor Wang Jie:**

I would like to say something about building a community with a shared future for humanity. General Secretary Xi Jinping pointed out that "*a single flower does not make a spring, while one hundred flowers in full bloom bring spring to the garden.*" Different countries have different ideologies and cultures. These differences are good points, they do not constitute superiority or inferiority.

There are two eye-catching slogans on the rostrum of Tiananmen Square: "*Long live the People's Republic of China*" and "*Long live the great unity of the people of the world*". So why are these two slogans placed in the heart of China, on the rostrum of Tiananmen? What is the significance behind it?

Isn't "*Long live the great unity of the people of the world*" the continuation of the Chinese ancient ideology of "*living in harmony with all others near and far*", "*myriad states enjoying repose*", "*all under heaven are one family"*, and *"living things that are nourished do not injure one another; roads that run parallel do not interfere with one another"*? The community with a shared future for humanity advocated by General Secretary Xi Jinping is a rational thought for the realisation of the great unity of the people of the world. Through our own efforts, China is pursuing the aspiration of the great unity of the people of the world. China will make new and greater contributions to humanity. China has confidence and will be more powerful!

Lightning Source UK Ltd.
Milton Keynes UK
UKHW040916051222
413416UK00005B/306